MARVEL

MUSEUM

STUDIO
PRESS

First published in the UK in 2019
by Studio Press Books,
part of Bonnier Books UK,
The Plaza, 535 King's Road,
London, SW10 0SZ

www.studiopressbooks.co.uk
www.bonnierbooks.co.uk

Printed in China
1 3 5 7 9 10 8 6 4 2

ISBN 978-178741-556-0

Written by Ned Hartley
Edited by Emma Drage
Designed by Rob Ward

Welcome to the

PREFACE

The secret to Marvel's success is no secret at all – Stan Lee was always very open about the fact that the element that separates the Marvel characters from all other super heroes is that they are people first and super heroes second.

As such, they grapple with the same sorts of everyday problems as their readers do – whether that's struggling to pay their rent, not being able to confess their feelings to the person they like or being unappreciated by a world they are trying to protect.

The colourful costumes and superhuman powers are all a part of the fantasy – the fun part, really. But the aspect that brings people back month in and month out to find out what will happen to their favourite character next is that human relatability. The Marvel heroes feel like people you know, and their struggles start to feel like your struggles – so when they're able to score a hard-fought victory, it's as cathartic and energising for you as it is for them!

A bonus – one the Marvel films are exploring today – is the fact that all of these different characters exist in the same world, so you never know exactly when the Hulk may show up to battle the Thing, or when Deadpool may toss a pie at Spider-Man. This interconnectivity means that while every Marvel story is a self-contained experience, together they all add up to something greater than the sum of its parts: The Marvel Universe!

This volume will give you a good overview of the main players in the Marvel Universe and the people who were responsible for creating them. But you've only scratched the surface. New wonderment awaits you every time you pick up a Marvel comic! Because once you crack open that cover – anything can happen!

Tom Brevoort
Executive Editor, Marvel

SECTION 1

SECRET ORIGINS

Marvel Comics #1
Timeline
Timely Comics – Namor, The Human Torch and Captain America

MARVEL COMICS #1

Marvel Comics #1 was a revelation – it was like no other comic that had ever been seen before. Published by Timely Publications, the cover was dated October 1939 and promised "ACTION, MYSTERY, ADVENTURE". The cover image, painted by science-fiction artist Frank R. Paul, depicted an otherworldly flaming man who didn't seem to mind that a bullet was being fired directly into his chest; in fact he was laughing! This was how readers met the first Human Torch.

Inside the comic, readers discovered that the Human Torch was a science experiment gone wrong – an android who had human feelings and emotions, but was cursed to burst into flames when he was exposed to oxygen. The creation of writer-artist Carl Burgos, the Human Torch's powers were as much of a curse as a blessing, and he struggled not to set fire to everyone around him. Still, the Human Torch was a bright, heroic character, and, despite being buried alive by his creator, he showed his humanity by dedicating his life to heroism. Right from the very beginning, Marvel characters were flawed, human and trying to do the right thing.

Namor the Sub-Mariner was definitely not human. Described by writer-artist Bill Everett in the opening caption box as "an ultra-man of the deep", Namor was a member of an underwater race of sub-mariners. Namor's story saw him almost immediately launch himself into a war against humanity, with the consequences of this war left open-ended.

Other comic strips included the jungle-based Ka-Zar the Great, the mustachioed Angel and the Western-themed Masked Raider, but it was the Human Torch and the Sub-Mariner who were clearly the freshest and most exciting characters.

The issue was a huge success, selling nearly 900,000 copies and laying part of the foundation for a new American art form. The first issue of *Marvel Comics* was a hit, meaning that more comics were going to be needed – and fast. Publisher Martin Goodman started to expand Timely Publishing, growing it into a company that would eventually become known to the world as Marvel Comics.

―――――――――――――― **KEY TO PLATE** ――――――――――――――

1: **Marvel Comics #1**
October 1939

The first appearance of the
original Human Torch, as well

as Namor the Sub-Mariner.

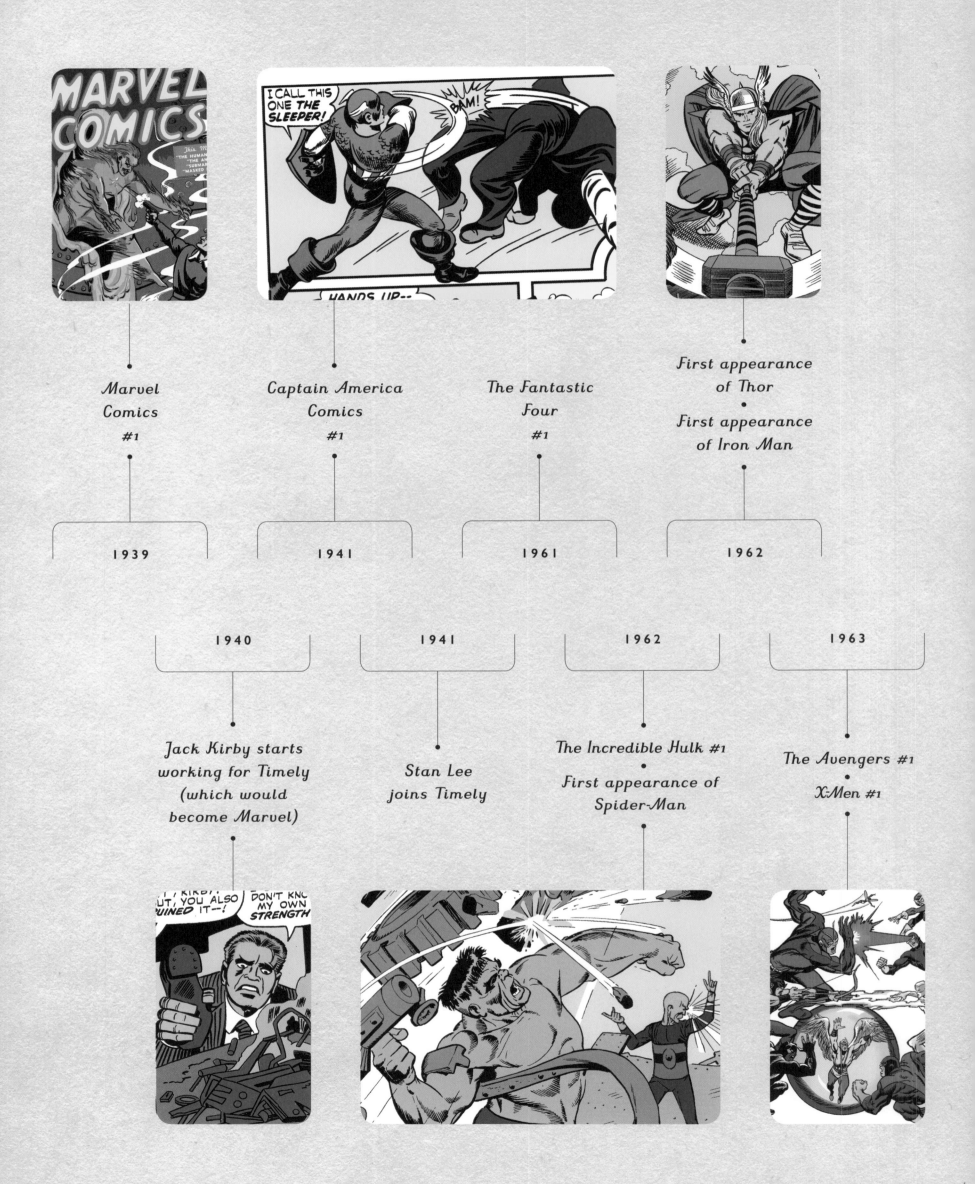

Marvel
Comics
#1

Captain America
Comics
#1

The Fantastic
Four
#1

First appearance
of Thor

First appearance
of Iron Man

1939

1941

1961

1962

1940

1941

1962

1963

Jack Kirby starts
working for Timely
(which would
become Marvel)

Stan Lee
joins Timely

The Incredible Hulk #1

First appearance of
Spider-Man

The Avengers #1

X-Men #1

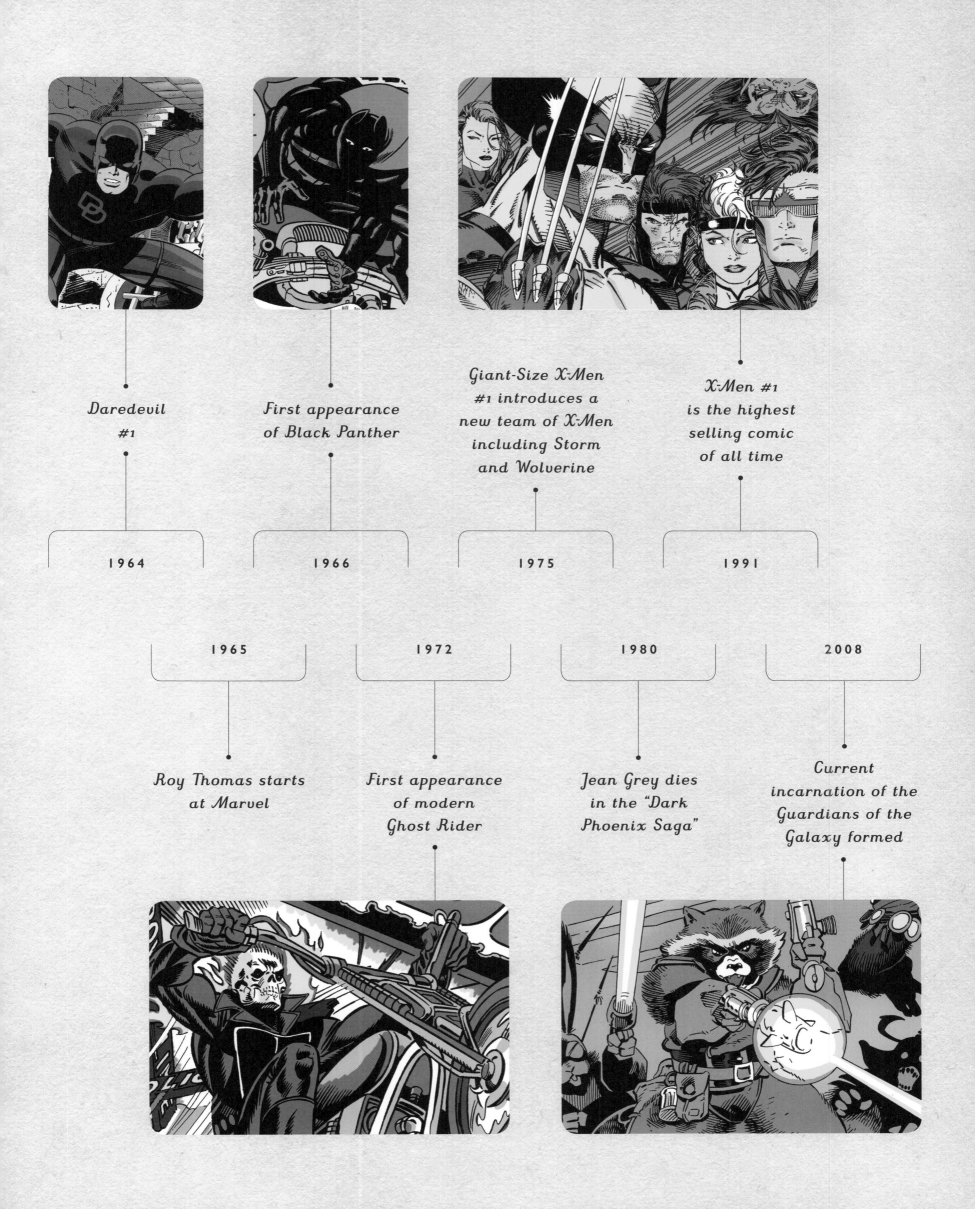

Daredevil #1

First appearance of Black Panther

Giant-Size X-Men #1 introduces a new team of X-Men including Storm and Wolverine

X-Men #1 is the highest selling comic of all time

1964

1966

1975

1991

1965

1972

1980

2008

Roy Thomas starts at Marvel

First appearance of modern Ghost Rider

Jean Grey dies in the "Dark Phoenix Saga"

Current incarnation of the Guardians of the Galaxy formed

TIMELY COMICS – NAMOR, THE HUMAN TORCH AND CAPTAIN AMERICA

Timely Comics soon became one of the biggest comics publishers around. Martin Goodman brought in Joe Simon and Jack Kirby as his editorial team to create more comics. *Marvel Comics* became *Marvel Mystery*, but the Human Torch and the Sub-Mariner stayed, even turning up in each other's stories in *Marvel Mystery #8*, and then fighting each other in issue #9 – the first Marvel crossover! Soon the Human Torch got his own comic, where he was joined by a kid sidekick called Toro, who was also unfortunate enough to be permanently on fire. Namor would also get his own title in 1941, but before that there was an even bigger comic to be launched.

Captain America Comics #1 was published at the same time as the rise of the Nazis in Germany. The cover of the first issue showed the title star punching Hitler in the face. Joe Simon and Jack Kirby produced a hero who was once a 90 pound weakling, but thanks to a "Super-Soldier Serum" was now a peak physical specimen. Helped by his sidekick Bucky (named after the star of Joe Simon's high school basketball team), Captain America brought a new level of patriotism to comics, and quickly became Timely's highest selling title – the second printing of issue #1 sold over a million copies. America couldn't get enough of the adventures of the star-spangled man! Though other heroes were introduced by Timely, none could match the popularity of Captain America, the Sub-Mariner and the Human Torch.

Martin Goodman needed an assistant to cope with the extra workload and his wife's young cousin needed work, so in 1941 young Stanley Lieber started work at Timely. When he wrote his first story a few months later called "Captain America Foils the Traitor's Revenge", he used a different name – Stan Lee. He kept this name, and Stan Lee has been part of the history of Marvel ever since.

The sheer range of comics that Timely produced in the 1940s was quite incredible. The super hero genre was popular during the war, but after World War II fashions changed. Readers wanted funny animal comics, and so titles like *Ziggy Pig, Silly Seal* and *Super Rabbit* started appearing. Timely wanted to create comics for everyone, so comics aimed at female readers like *Nellie the Nurse* and *Tessie the Typist* were launched in the 1940s. Stan Lee and Martin Goodman were determined to give the public whatever they wanted and always to be one step ahead of the competition!

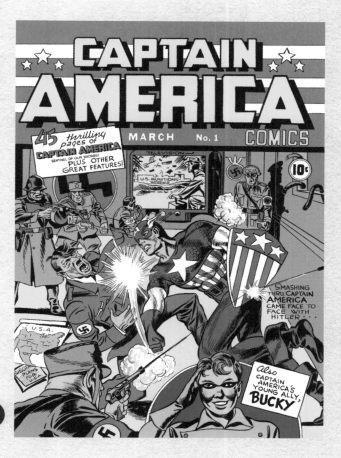

KEY TO PLATE

1: Marvel Mystery Comics #9
July 1940
Namor and the Human Torch clash
in the first Marvel crossover.

2: Marvel Mystery Comics #15
January 1941
The Human Torch and the
Sub-Mariner soon became allies
and teamed up to fight the Nazis.

3: Captain America Comics #1
March 1941
Steve Rogers, Captain America,

was first introduced to readers in
this issue.

4: Captain America Comics #1
March 1941
Captain America was often aided
by his young ally, Bucky.

COSMIC RAYS!

Atlas Comics
Stan Lee
Jack Kirby
The Fantastic Four

ATLAS COMICS

In 1951 comics that had been published under Timely started using the name Atlas on the cover, and the company moved their offices to the 14th floor of the Empire State Building. Super hero comics had fallen out of fashion, and they stopped publishing super hero comics with *Captain America* #75. Cap, Namor and the Human Torch would appear a few times in the 1950s, but were not as popular as they had been in the previous decade.

Atlas Comics followed trends in TV and movies, so when Westerns and monster movies were popular Atlas created *Two-Gun Kid*, *Western Outlaws* and *Mystery Tales*. Soon humour comics were fashionable, so Atlas produced comics like *Millie the Model* (which would run until the 1970s) and *Patsy Walker* (who would later become Marvel's Hellcat). When readers wanted funny animal comics then *Dippy Duck*, *Marvin Mouse* and *The Monkey and the Bear* were produced. Horror comics like *Adventures into Terror* and *Strange Tales* were all especially popular with readers at the start of the 1950s.

In 1954 US senators publicly blamed comics for crime and juvenile delinquency, so publishers came together to create the Comics Code Authority, which limited what could be shown in comics, restricting which stories and situations could be used. Then, in the mid-1950s, distribution problems meant that Atlas went from producing between 40 to 60 books a month to producing eight. Around the same time Martin Goodman discovered a huge trove of unpublished but completed art, enough to keep Atlas going for months. Nearly all of the staff at Atlas Comics were laid off; there were no pencillers, letterers or inkers any more. Stan Lee was virtually the only person to keep his job.

Atlas did start creating comics again, but now the artists were all freelancers, paid by the page, rather than being regular, full-time staff members. Stan worried about keeping his best artists in work, but thankfully Jack Kirby, Bill Everett and a newcomer called Steve Ditko were keen to create comics. Titles like *Journey Into Mystery*, *Tales to Astonish* and *Tales of Suspense* told lurid stories of Martians, mummies and monsters. These stories were doing well, but at the start of the 1960s super hero comics started to come back into fashion, and everything changed...

─────────────── **KEY TO PLATE** ───────────────

1: Tales of Suspense #1
January 1959

This cover art by Don Heck shows the kind of exciting science fiction

stories that were popular in the late 1950s.

IND.
TALES OF SUSPENSE
APPROVED BY THE COMICS CODE AUTHORITY
1 JAN.
10¢
BACK TO THE SHIP! THE THING IS INDESTRUCTIBLE!
WHERE DID IT COME FROM? WHAT *IS* IT?
DON HECK
"I DARED TO EXPLORE THE UNKNOWN EMPTINESS!"

STAN LEE

Stan Lee is a household name, famous for co-creating some of the most incredible and exciting characters of the 20th century. His boundless enthusiasm, warmth and creativity have inspired generations, giving countless readers a new way of looking at the world. But before Stan created these iconic stories, he was almost ready to give up comics entirely.

Stan Lee grew up as the son of immigrant parents in Manhattan. His father was a dress cutter, but found it hard to get work during the Great Depression. Stan always claimed that he learned a great lesson from his father's hardship and promised to work as hard as he could to make sure that he didn't suffer the same fate. When Stan was eight his younger brother Larry was born, and the two brothers shared a room for much of their childhood. Larry later followed Stan into comics, and wrote many stories for Marvel.

Stan entered the army in 1942 and first served in the Signal Corps, but was later given the military designation of "playwright", which involved writing training manuals and educational material. Stan was still writing for Timely while in the army, and would send back comic scripts every week. After the war, Stan returned to Timely Comics and stayed in Manhattan, and in 1947 he met Joan Boocock, a British model. Stan would consistently recount that he fell in love with her immediately, and proposed to her after only two weeks of dating. The two were married, and in 1950 their daughter Joan Celia "J.C." Lee was born, all while Stan was working at Timely and later Atlas Comics.

By 1961 Stan Lee was disillusioned with comics and wanted to quit. He loved working with his artists and revered the work of Jack Kirby, but he wanted something more. Stan had always dreamed of writing "the Great American Novel", and one of the reasons that he hadn't used his real name in comics was that he didn't want his comics work associated with the highbrow book he intended to write one day. Stan's wife Joan suggested that he use the modern, realistic characters that he wanted to use in his books in his comics. Stan agreed and comics were changed forever.

Stan's amazing creativity and enthusiasm allowed him to form a whole new universe in just a few short years. Working with a team of incredible collaborators, he was able to co-create heartfelt stories that linked and played off each other in ways that wouldn't be possible in any other medium.

KEY TO PLATE

JACK KIRBY

If there is a signature look that defined Marvel comics in the 1960s, it comes from the pencil of Jack Kirby. While other artists made huge contributions to Marvel, there is only one creator who was given the nickname "King".

Jack Kirby was five years older than Stan Lee, and like Stan he was a New Yorker born to Jewish parents. Born Jacob Kurtzberg, he never took any formal art lessons, taking inspiration from any comic strips that he could find. He worked on newspaper comic strips, and after a brief stint in animation moved to monthly comics. Jacob Kurtzberg dabbled with a few pen names such as Curt Davis, Ted Grey and Lance Kirby before eventually arriving at Jack Kirby. Jack joined Timely Comics in 1940, where he created *Captain America* with Joe Simon, which became one of the decade's biggest hits.

Jack met Roz Goldstein in 1941. They married in 1942 but a year later Jack was drafted into the army. During World War II Jack served in the Infantry, and because of his art skills he was often sent as a scout behind enemy lines to draw maps and enemy positions. He used what he saw in the war in his comics, and that is perhaps part of the reason that his action scenes are so realistic, but also feel so dangerous.

After the war Jack worked for a number of different comic book companies, partnering with Joe Simon in many different genres. Jack worked on *Young Romance* for Prize Comics, a comic which promised "all true love stories" on the cover – this was the first romance

comic and is often credited with creating a whole new comics genre. He eventually returned to working for Timely (which was now Atlas Comics), working on supernatural and science fiction; his speciality was stories where giant monsters attacked helpless cities.

Jack's incredible work ethic and levels of productivity meant that he was a legend in the comics industry. He would work for 12 to 14 hours a day in his house in Long Island, producing four to five pages of exciting and dynamic comic artwork every day, while some artists struggled to complete one. Kirby's prolific page rate meant that he could pencil several comics every month, giving the early Marvel comics' line a style of its own.

Marvel wouldn't be Marvel without Jack Kirby. He created so much of the look, the feel and the emotion of early Marvel heroes that it is impossible to imagine the current age of super heroes without him. Kirby's heroes are natural and completely stylised at the same time – they are gods with human problems.

--------- **KEY TO PLATE** ---------

1: **What If? Vol 1 #11**
October 1978
No image of Jack Kirby is complete without his signature cigar.

2: **The Avengers #4**
March 1964
In 1964 Jack Kirby returned to *Captain America*, when Steve Rogers was added to the Avengers' roster.

3: **The Avengers #1**
September 1963
In his iconic panel, the Wasp gives the Avengers their name, bringing the team together.

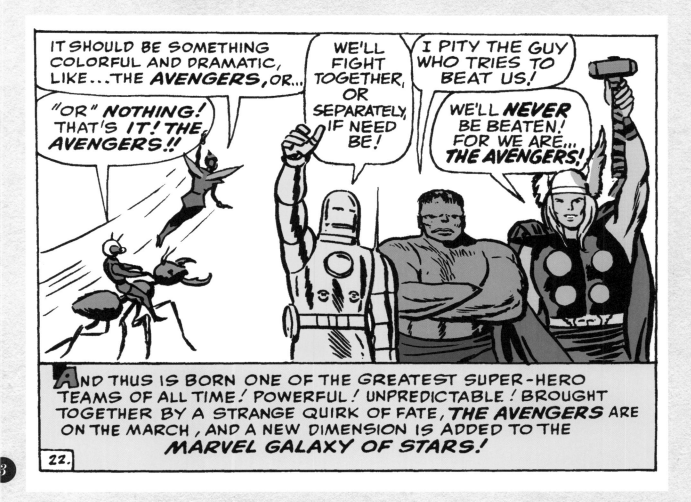

THE FANTASTIC FOUR

There is a comics industry legend that publisher Martin Goodman was playing golf with one of the publishers of DC comics, who told him that their biggest selling book was the *Justice League*, and that readers wanted team super hero books. Whether this is true or not, Goodman certainly asked Stan Lee to create a team super hero book in 1961. The result was the flawed, human, bickering heroes of the Fantastic Four, whose humanity and relatability would set the mould for comics for decades to come. These heroes were not unrealistic archetypes, they were real people with genuine problems.

"The toughest thing about doing any super hero series is producing the very first issue," Stan Lee would later write. "If the introductory story doesn't grab the readers the chances are they won't come back for the subsequent issues."[1] Stan knew that he needed his best artist on the job, and Jack Kirby was only too happy to deliver. Jack's time spent drawing monster comics is evident on the cover of *The Fantastic Four #1*. The main image is of a misshapen giant forcing its way out of the earth, screaming directly at the reader. Around him, a series of strange figures prepare to battle the beast, but how will they stop him?

When readers opened the comic, the story inside was new and unsettling. Four figures were called together to meet an initially unspecified menace, but these were no ordinary heroes – they seemed to cause as many problems as they solved. The invisible Sue Storm caused a commotion downtown, the hulking Ben Grimm smashed his way through New York, and the flaming Johnny Storm was targeted by the National Guard.

The Fantastic Four were astronauts, bombarded with cosmic rays, which gave them incredible powers. Reed Richards could now stretch his body into impossible lengths, while his girlfriend Sue Storm could turn invisible at will. Sue's brother Johnny could cover his whole body in flames, while pilot Ben Grimm was transformed into a super-strong rock creature. These were heroes who were fallible, who fought and argued with each other, and who sounded more realistic and more human than anyone in super hero comics had before.

Stan knew that *The Fantastic Four* was a hit when letters started pouring in, and he added a letter column to the third issue. Interacting with fans would be vital to Marvel's success, as well as being a useful way of gauging feedback on these new types of super hero stories.

Namor the Sub-Mariner returned to comics in *The Fantastic Four #4*, every bit as unhappy with mankind as the last time that readers saw him. Stan and Jack started playing with longer, more involved storylines that would take several issues to complete, because the adventures of Reed, Ben, Johnny and Sue became so intricate and complex that a single issue couldn't contain them. This was a new art form, a type of storytelling that had never been seen in comics before, which took inspiration from heroic myths as much as it did daily soap operas.

The Fantastic Four have evolved over the years – Reed and Susan have had children, while Ben and Johnny have at least tried to settle down. But the popularity of the comic comes from the deep bonds of family, something that will never grow old.

--- **KEY TO PLATE** ---

1: **The Fantastic Four #1**
November 1961
Jack Kirby's incredible cover to *The Fantastic Four #1* shows his skill in drawing monster comics.

2: **The Fantastic Four #1**
November 1961
Jack Kirby and Stan Lee knew how to start a comic with intrigue.

3: **The Fantastic Four #1**
November 1961
Johnny Storm, the new Human Torch, was not related to the previous character with the same name. He would soon become just as popular.

4: **The Fantastic Four #52**
July 1966
Stan Lee and Jack Kirby created a huge range of characters in the pages of *The Fantastic Four*, including Silver Surfer, Galactus and Black Panther.

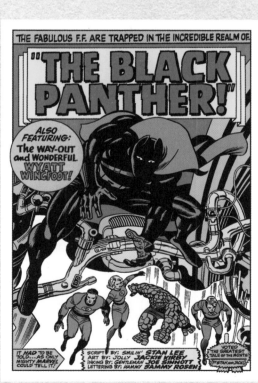

SECTION 3

AVENGERS ASSEMBLE!

THE INCREDIBLE HULK

Stan Lee had plans for a whole universe of new and realistic characters, all living in the same world. *The Incredible Hulk* #1 was released in 1962 – A Dr Jekyll and Mr Hyde-like story, where brainy scientist Bruce Banner rushed to save a delinquent youth from a gamma bomb and got caught in the explosion, transforming himself into a rampaging beast. Stan was building a story around ideas that were in the news at the time – the Hulk could very much be seen as the walking personification of anxiety about the nuclear bomb.

The noble savagery of the Hulk was something that always interested Stan Lee. "I've always had a soft spot in my heart for the Frankenstein monster," Stan would later remember. "No one could ever convince me he was the bad guy. He never wanted to hurt anyone; he merely groped his torturous way through a second life trying to defend himself, trying to come to terms with those who sought to destroy him."[2]

Jack Kirby's brooding pencils managed to capture the energy and horror of an atomic bomb explosion as well as the power and pain of the Hulk himself. Though the Hulk was grey in the first issue, production processes couldn't keep that colour consistent through the comic, so he was changed to green in *The Incredible Hulk* #2.

The savage Hulk wasn't initially as big a hit as the Fantastic Four. Perhaps the comic-buying public wasn't quite ready for such a powerful character, even though he would become hugely popular a few years later. Issues one to five were pencilled by Jack Kirby and issue six was pencilled and inked by Steve Ditko, who suggested that Banner should turn into the Hulk when he was angry, not just at night.

After five decades the Hulk is one of the most recognisable super heroes of all time. Like every Marvel hero, the Hulk has transformed over the years – he's been a Las Vegas bouncer, a super-smart professor and even an intergalactic warrior champion. Stan Lee's initial pitch to Jack Kirby was that the Hulk should be an "attractive monster" and the character always returns to that core idea.

─────────── **KEY TO PLATE** ───────────

*1: **The Incredible Hulk #1***
May 1962
"Is he Man or Monster, or... Is he Both?" This question is at the centre of all the best Hulk stories.

*2: **The Incredible Hulk #1***
May 1962
The Hulk was grey in his first appearance, but was green in later issues. He would revert to grey again, in a new identity many years later.

*3: **The Incredible Hulk #2***
July 1962
Jack Kirby always gave the Hulk a noble, haunted look.

*4: **The Incredible Hulk #6***
March 1963
Spider-Man artist Steve Ditko drew the Hulk briefly in 1963.

20

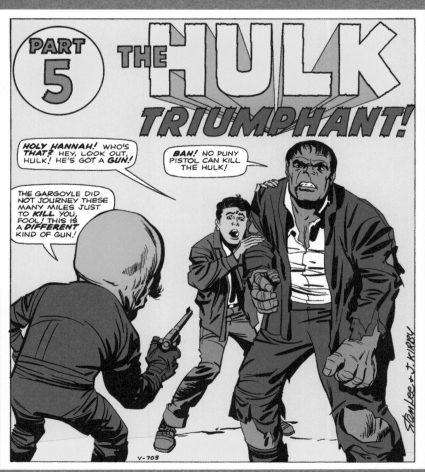

THE MIGHTY THOR

Jack Kirby loved ancient myths and legends, and he wanted to update them for the modern era. A version of Thor had been seen in Marvel comics before, appearing in *Venus*, a 1951 comic about the goddess of love and romance, but this toga-clad figure was very different from the thunder god that Jack Kirby, Stan Lee and Larry Lieber were about to unleash on the world.

The cover of *Journey Into Mystery* #83 promised, as many of Stan Lee's comics did, "the most exciting super hero of all time!" Disabled doctor Donald Blake, pursued by alien rock-monsters, finds a wooden stick which turns him into the Norse god Thor, a rippling specimen of physical perfection. The damaged Doctor Blake would seem to be a better fit for the new, relatable stories that Marvel was trying to tell than the near-perfect Asgardian, but Don was eventually revealed to be an aspect of Thor's personality created by Thor's father, Odin.

Thor's speech patterns sounded like no other Marvel hero. "When I wrote Thor's early stories," said Stan Lee, "I felt it wouldn't be right to simply have him talk like any ordinary Joe... So I borrowed some phraseology from the Bible, from Shakespeare and from *The Rubáiyát of Omar Khayyám*. I added plenty of my own far-out expressions and, lo and behold, Thor-Speak was born!"[3]

Jack Kirby's Asgard was classic, modern and eternal all at the same time, with golden towers looming over the rainbow bridge to Midgard (Earth). Readers were taken on fantastic voyages between worlds, with only Jack Kirby's strong visual storytelling style and Stan Lee's distinctive dialogue to guide them. One of the comic's strengths was Thor's wide cast of supporting characters – Jack Kirby's fascination with Norse mythology paid off as Thor was joined by his treacherous brother Loki, his omnipotent father Odin, and friends Heimdall, Sif and the Warriors Three. Thor's story became an epic saga as he bounced between worlds, defying orders from his father so that he could try to be with his love, Jane Foster.

The true power of *The Mighty Thor* was that it was always part Norse mythology and part soap opera. Stan and Jack knew that readers wouldn't care about Asgard if they didn't care about Thor and Jane Foster first. Thor's stories are not about Asgard, but about the Asgardians and the lives they touch.

KEY TO PLATE

1: **Journey Into Mystery #83**
August 1962
Jack Kirby's dynamic artwork gave Thor a modern feel.

2: **Journey Into Mystery #83**
August 1962
In his first appearance, Thor saves the Earth from the Stone Men from Saturn.

3: **Journey Into Mystery #86**
November 1962
Thor soon became popular and was pitted against science fiction enemies.

4: **Journey Into Mystery #104**
May 1964
Thor is surrounded by the faces of Odin, Balder, Surtur, Skagg the Storm Giant and Loki.

THE INVINCIBLE IRON MAN

Tales of Suspense #39 introduced Iron Man, the alter ego of industrialist, inventor, weapons manufacturer and playboy Tony Stark, who was captured during the Vietnam War and forced to make an iron suit of armour to protect himself. Fellow prisoner and scientist Ho Yinsen helped Tony create the armour, but died helping Tony escape.

Marvel characters tended to have a fatal flaw and Tony Stark was no exception; a piece of shrapnel was lodged in his chest, constantly trying to burrow its way into his heart – the invulnerability of his exterior suit of armour contrasting with his wounded interior. Tony Stark himself was a rakish, Howard Hughes-like figure, whose playboy lifestyle and quick wit was just as much a defence mechanism as the repulsors on his armour. The first appearance of Iron Man was plotted by Stan Lee and scripted by Larry Lieber, the character was designed by Jack Kirby and the story was drawn by Don Heck. The first time readers saw Iron Man's armour it was a slightly boxy, grey affair, but in later appearances Kirby's initial design was reinvented by Steve Ditko as a sleeker and more stylish red-and-gold outfit.

Iron Man's early battles involved lots of Russians and communists, with his rogues' gallery featuring villains including Black Widow, Titanium Man and the Crimson Dynamo. Tony also had to fight his own self-destructive and alcoholic tendencies which would be addressed in the groundbreaking "Demon in a Bottle" storyline. Tony's humanity, complexity and ingenuity have delighted fans for years.

As it is always on the forefront of modern technology, Tony's Iron Man armour has changed more than any other super hero costume. Iron Man has had space suits, underwater suits, nanotechnology suits, Hulkbuster suits and invisible suits. He has given a suit of armour to his best friend James "Rhodey" Rhodes, who now uses it as the hero War Machine. Iron Man's popularity doesn't come from the armour, but because under that armour lies a damaged and very human heart.

———————————————— **KEY TO PLATE** ————————————————

1: *Tales of Suspense* #39
March 1963
Early versions of the Iron Man armour had a radio antennae on the shoulder.

2: *Tales of Suspense* #39
March 1963
Iron Man's armour looked very different in his first appearance.

3: *Tales of Suspense* #48
December 1963
Iron Man's red-and-gold costume was designed by Steve Ditko and was first seen in this cover by Jack Kirby.

4: *Tales of Suspense* #48
December 1963
The new red-and-gold armour was lighter, putting less of a strain on Tony Stark's heart.

5: *Tales of Suspense* #82
October 1966

6: *Tales of Suspense* #95
November 1967
Iron Man's repulsor rays are a vital part of the character's armoury.

ANT-MAN AND THE WASP

Marvel already had the biggest heroes in the world, so by 1962 it was time to find the smallest ones. Hank Pym had already appeared in *Tales to Astonish* #27, and *Tales to Astonish* #35 promised readers they would "Gasp in amazement at the return of the Ant-Man!" In a story by Stan Lee and Jack Kirby, biophysicist Dr Hank Pym had previously developed a serum (which he named Pym Particles) that allowed him to shrink to the size of an ant. After being chased around a teeming ant hill, Hank returned to normal size and vowed to put Pym Particles to good use. Constructing a helmet and suit that allowed him to communicate with ants, he became Ant-Man! Almost immediately, criminals got in the way, and trenchcoated Russians invaded Pym's lab looking for an anti-radiation formula. Hank was locked in his lab, but managed to use his Pym Particles to shrink down and then use an army of ants to save the day.

Ant-Man soon gained a partner in *Tales to Astonish* #44, in the form of Janet van Dyne – the Wasp. When Hank first met Janet he was mourning his first wife, Maria Trovaya. Janet was the daughter of Hank's scientist colleague Vernon van Dyne, and

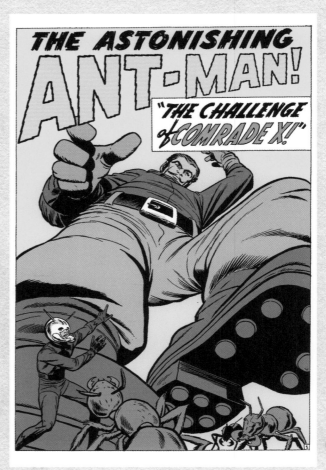

she too suffered a loss when her father was murdered. Seeing Janet's determination to find her father's murderer, Hank took her as a super hero partner, giving her subdermal wings and antennae that would only appear when she shrunk down to become the Wasp. Stan obviously felt that Ant-Man needed some romantic tension, because the two characters did not become lovers for years.

The Wasp was a popular addition to the title, but Stan Lee continued to tinker with Ant-Man, giving him the ability to grow in size and renaming him Giant-Man. Janet's sense of style and fashion won many fans' hearts, and her costume revamps became part of her character. Janet has had more costumes than anyone else in the Marvel Universe, and later became a costume designer for other heroes.

Though they never gained their own title, Ant-Man and the Wasp shared *Tales to Astonish* with a revived and increasingly popular Hulk. Most importantly, Hank and Janet were founding members of the Avengers. Ant-Man and the Wasp have been core Avengers members since the start, and have been involved in most incarnations of the team.

KEY TO PLATE

1: Tales to Astonish #35
September 1962
Hank Pym's special helmet allowed him to communicate with ants and control them!

2: Tales to Astonish #36
October 1962
The relative size of Ant-Man allowed

Jack Kirby to produce some incredible visual effects.

3: Tales to Astonish #44
June 1963
Janet van Dyne was introduced to the comic a few issues later and immediately assumed the identity of the Wasp.

4: Tales to Astonish #44
June 1963
Ant-Man gave the Wasp her super hero identity.

CAPTAIN AMERICA

Part of creating a super hero universe meant looking back to see what had worked before. Stan had already included Namor and (a completely different) Human Torch in the Fantastic Four, but there was a Timely Comics stalwart who was waiting in the wings – the star-spangled man himself. Stan had already teased readers about a possible return of Cap in *Strange Tales* #114 in 1963, where the Fantastic Four's Johnny Storm met a circus performing Captain America who was revealed to be villain the Acrobat in disguise. Letters flowed in; fans wanted the *real* Captain America back.

The Avengers #4 showed that Captain America had fallen from a plane in the final days of World War II and had been frozen in a block of ice ever since. Steve Rogers was now a fish out of water, trying to understand the 1960s society which was fundamentally different from the wartime nation that he had left.

Readers could catch up with the modern-day Captain America in *The Avengers* then read new World War II adventures by Stan and Jack in *Tales of Suspense*, including a retelling of Cap's origin. Bucky returned in these flashback comics, and so did Red Skull who was still getting his orders from the Fuehrer himself.

Soon Steve Rogers' stories moved to the present day, and rather than seem like a relic of a different age, he became a useful way of looking at contemporary ideas. *Captain America* addressed racism when the comic introduced the Falcon, one of the first African-American super heroes, and for a while the comic was renamed *Captain America and the Falcon*. Steve has always had a powerful moral code, taking on everyone from Iron Man to the President and not backing down. Penciller Gene Colan knew exactly what made Cap great when he started drawing him: "Captain America represented this country's image of what a hero should be," said Colan. "I [knew] in my heart it was not so much his words or actions, but what he stood for I respected."[4]

―――――――――――――― **KEY TO PLATE** ――――――――――――――

1: **Tales of Suspense**
November 1964
In these stories Captain America was often outnumbered, but never outmatched!

2: **Captain America #117**
September 1969
In 1969 Cap was joined by the Falcon, Sam Wilson, and his bird, Redwing.

3: **Captain America #193**
January 1976
Jack Kirby produced some of the most dynamic and exciting covers of his career while working on *Captain America*.

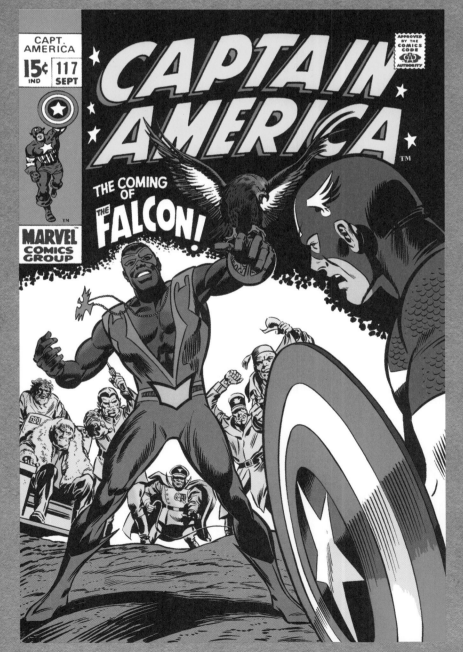

BLACK PANTHER

Debuting in *Fantastic Four* #52 in 1966, the Black Panther appeared in comics several months before the political movement of the same name. T'Challa was one of the earliest black super heroes in comics, and was the first with any powers. To put this in context, the Voting Rights Act which guaranteed African-Americans the right to vote, had only been passed one year earlier in 1965. Co-creators Stan Lee and Jack Kirby worked hard to try to keep the character away from racial caricatures or stereotypes.

T'Challa was the king of the fictional African nation of Wakanda, a technologically advanced utopia where the scientific inventions surpassed even those of Reed Richards. Jack Kirby was the master at creating visually astounding science fiction environments, and his Wakanda is a precise jungle of advanced wires and cables – everything in the nation is joined together like the motherboard of some giant computer.

As with many super hero encounters, T'Challa ended up fighting the Fantastic Four when they first met, but he later became their ally. Black Panther teamed up with Captain America a few years later in 1968 when T'Challa brought Steve Rogers to Wakanda to help him battle Baron Zemo. That same year Black Panther came to New York and in *The Avengers* #52 he joined the Earth's mightiest heroes, and has been involved with the team in some way ever since.

The Black Panther was revealed to be the title given to the chief of the Panther Tribe of Wakanda, and was held before by T'Challa's father, T'Chaka. Over the years other characters have also held this title, including T'Challa's sister Shuri, after T'Challa was injured in battle.

Throughout his career T'Challa has continued to be an inspiration. Black Panther writer Reginald Hudlin explained this, writing: "For black readers, the unprecedented nature of the character was shocking… The idea of a black super hero who was a king of a kingdom with incredible wealth and scientific genius that somehow perfectly balanced its own cultural legacy with the best of the Western World… who could imagine that but Stan and Jack? To write such a character with no superpowers but introducing him to us by having him defeat the Fantastic Four – in their own book?… Captain America represented the best of the American Spirit. The Black Panther represented the best of the African Spirit. There is no other character that represents an entire continent with such class and dignity."[5]

KEY TO PLATE

1: Fantastic Four #52
July 1966
T'Challa fought the Fantastic Four in his first appearance, and nearly beat them.

2: Fantastic Four #52
July 1966

3: Tales of Suspense #98
February 1968

4: Tales of Suspense #98
February 1968
Before joining the Avengers, Black Panther teamed up with Captain America.

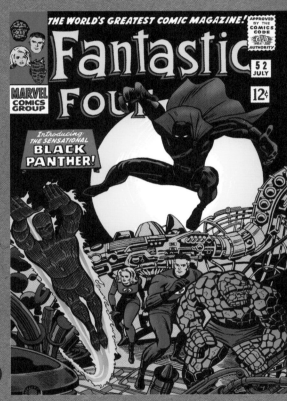

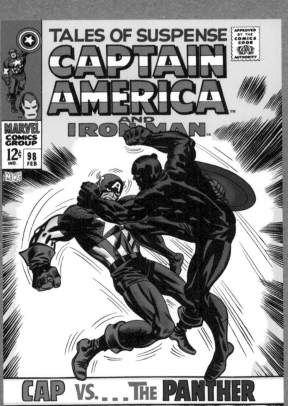

BLACK WIDOW

When Black Widow first appeared as an Iron Man villain in *Tales of Suspense* #52 in 1964, she wasn't a super hero, but a spy. She was under orders from her Russian superiors to team up with the Crimson Dynamo to destroy Stark and a Russian defector named Professor Vanko – Natasha failed to kill Stark but Vanko died in a fight with the Crimson Dynamo. "Madame Natasha" reappeared several times as a femme fatale character, playing on Tony's weakness for beautiful women. She even convinced Hawkeye to attack Iron Man in *Tales of Suspense* #57, several months before both characters became heroes instead of villains.

"Even though she started as a villainess and I later tried to make her a heroine, I've always secretly suspected that she was more interesting as a wicked woman than a law-abiding lady," explained Stan Lee. "But she was fun to write about because I could always keep the reader guessing as to whether to like her or loathe her. Although, as far as I'm concerned, the lady was too lovely to loathe no matter what she did."[6]

Black Widow finally got a costume and weapons in *The Avengers* #29 but she was still trying to kill Iron Man and the Avengers. Thankfully, her love for Hawkeye meant that she was able to break her Russian conditioning and defect to America in the following issue. Natasha wouldn't officially join the Avengers until *The Avengers* #111, many years later.

The Amazing Spider-Man #86 saw Black Widow drop her pointed mask and adopt the red hair, black catsuit and wrist-shooters look that has defined the super hero

ever since. While Natasha has no superpowers she has extensive KGB espionage and combat training, along with an extensive set of spy gadgets and weapons. For several years Black Widow teamed up with Daredevil and for 16 issues *Daredevil* became *Daredevil and the Black Widow*. Natasha and Matt Murdock eventually parted ways, and she has been a key member of the Avengers ever since.

The Avengers is a team of human and conflicted heroes, often struggling to do the right thing and to listen to the voices of their better angels. Black Widow's story has always been about mistakes, forgiveness and repentance — there are many Avengers who have made poor choices in their previous lives, and there is nothing more heroic than striving to be a better person.

───────────── **KEY TO PLATE** ─────────────

1: **Tales of Suspense #53**
May 1964
Black Widow originally called herself "Madame Natasha" and schemed against Tony Stark.

2: **The Avengers #29**
June 1966
Black Widow's first costume was very different to the black catsuit she would later wear.

3: **The Amazing Spider-Man #86**
July 1970
Natasha's current outfit was debuted when she fought Spider-Man, trying to get the secret to his powers.

THE AVENGERS

Stan Lee had been playing the long game, slowly seeding different heroes throughout the fledgling universe that he and his collaborators had been creating. By the end of 1963, it was time to pull everything together. It was time for *The Avengers #1*.

In the story titled "The Coming of the Avengers", Thor's evil brother Loki framed the Hulk for a crime that he did not commit. In the course of the story, Thor, Iron Man, Ant-Man and the Wasp all join forces with Hulk to clear his name. They fight at first, but eventually they learn to work together to defeat Loki, with a jubilant Wasp naming the team in the final panel of the story. Writer Stan Lee and penciller Jack Kirby had a hand in creating all the characters in the Avengers' roster, so keeping them thematically and visually consistent was not a problem. For readers this really did feel as if all their favourite heroes were coming together for the first time.

It's fascinating to hear Stan Lee explain why he thought the different personalities of the Avengers worked so well together: "Iron Man's alter ego, the wealthy industrialist Tony Stark, was a natural leader. Don Blake, in the persona of Thor, Son of Odin, provided the necessary colour and contrast as well as a fabulous sense of fantasy. Henry Pym and his lady-love, Jan, were totally different from the others that they rounded the team out beautifully. As for the Hulk, any group of do-gooders that included a not-so-jolly green giant would never have a dull moment."[7]

Part of the thrill of the Avengers came from the team's ever-changing roster. In issue #2 Ant-Man started to use Pym Particles to grow in size and called himself Giant-Man. The Hulk left the team in the same issue, but returned to team up with Namor to fight the Avengers in the next issue. World War II living legend Captain America filled the Hulk's place in the roster from issue #4.

Membership of the team was stable until *The Avengers #16* when every member except Captain America left the team. Cap recruited former villains Hawkeye, Quicksilver and the Scarlet Witch to fill the Avengers' ranks. Over the next few years the roster would expand to include Black Widow, Black Knight and Black Panther among others. Soon they were joined by the Vision, a synthetic android created by the villainous Ultron, who would break his programming and fall in love with the Scarlet Witch. As the Avengers grew, so did the scope of their adventures. Before long they were battling the Squadron Supreme in alternate dimensions, or caught in the middle of galactic conflicts in the Kree-Skrull War. The Avengers were bigger than the world.

─────────────── **KEY TO PLATE** ───────────────

1: **The Avengers #1**
September 1963
In the first Avengers issue Loki framed Hulk for a crime he did not commit.

2: **The Avengers Annual #1**
September 1967
The original Avengers members would often return to the team in further adventures.

3: **The Avengers #16**
May 1965
A new team featuring Quicksilver, Hawkeye and the Scarlet Witch replaced the original roster.

SECTION 4

SPIDER-SENSE TINGLING!

Steve Ditko
Spider-Man
Doctor Strange
Daredevil

STEVE DITKO

In many ways, the reclusive Steve Ditko was the polar opposite of the bombastic Stan Lee. Steve came from a small town in Pennsylvania, while Stan was a New Yorker. Steve had always wanted to create comics, while Stan dreamed of being a great novelist. Stan loved giving interviews, while Steve only wanted to communicate through his work. Stan's stories included liberal ideas, while Steve became more enamoured of Ayn Rand's objectivist and libertarian ideas. But something about the alchemy between these two men created the most popular super hero the world has ever seen.

Born in 1927 in Johnstown, Pennsylvania, Steve loved comics from an early age, collecting *Prince Valiant* comics and sharing them with his father as a child. As soon as he was able, Steve moved to New York, studying under Batman artist Jerry Robinson at the Cartoonists and Illustrators School. Steve's determination and raw talent got him work with a variety of different comics companies, but his career in comics was nearly cut short when he contracted a severe bout of tuberculosis in 1954 and was forced to return home to Pennsylvania to recuperate. When Steve had recovered, Stan Lee was impressed with his work and gave him regular offbeat science fiction short story comics. Stan particularly liked working with Steve because he worked so well with the "Marvel Method" of writing, where Stan would give the artist brief plot outlines, and let them block in the artwork as they saw fit.

Steve's art style was so dramatic and expressive that it was like no one else at the time. Steve spent hours studying, and would keep books of reference material by his work desk so that he could draw everything exactly right — from the folds in a woman's dress to the shape of the gun in an alien's hands.

Stan and Steve were working on *Amazing Adult Fantasy* — the title was chosen to make readers feel sophisticated. Stan wanted a new super hero, but one who felt new and exciting, an ordinary teen who would resonate with Marvel's growing teenage readership. He already had a name… Spider-Man!

KEY TO PLATE

1: Amazing Adult Fantasy #12
May 1962
Steve Ditko could create troubled and tormented characters like no other artist.

2: Amazing Adult Fantasy #14
July 1962
Steve Ditko and Stan Lee worked together for years before the birth of Spider-Man.

3: Amazing Fantasy #15
August 1962
In Spider-Man's origin story, Steve Ditko gave Peter Parker a nervous, anxious quality.

4: The Amazing Spider-Man Annual #1
October 1964
This self-portrait of Steve Ditko possibly shows his studio at the time.

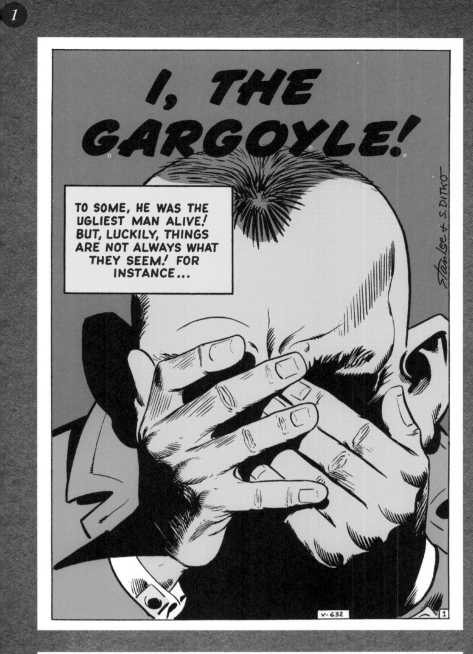

SPIDER-MAN

Stan Lee didn't go to Steve Ditko at first when he was looking for an artist for Spider-Man; he went to Jack Kirby. Stan wanted a young, relatable super hero, but when Jack Kirby produced pages about a boy who found a magic ring that gave him spider powers, they just weren't quite right. They weren't bad; they just weren't what Stan was looking for. So he approached Steve Ditko.

Steve had very set ideas about how Spider-Man should look and feel; he wanted this comic to be faithful and accurate to teenage life. Peter Parker wasn't a strapping Kirby-like super hero, he was a slight figure who often slunk into the shadows.

Amazing Fantasy #15 (renamed from *Amazing Adult Fantasy* for its final issue) told the story of Peter Parker, a bookish teenager who was bitten by a radioactive spider, giving him incredible powers. At first Peter used his powers to make money, but when a burglar that he could have stopped killed his uncle Ben, Peter vowed to become a hero. The story ends with the final panel reminding us that "With great power there must come – great responsibility!"

Publisher Martin Goodman was not at all sure about the character who would later become Marvel's most popular hero, and only agreed to include Spider-Man because this was the last issue of a cancelled comic. "We were about to discontinue our *Amazing Fantasy* series," wrote Stan Lee. "That meant nobody would care what stories I put into it, because it would be the last issue anyway." Martin Goodman soon changed his mind when sales of the comic shot through the roof, and by early 1963 Spidey had his own regular title – *The Amazing Spider-Man*.

One of the many things that fans loved about Spider-Man was his humanity. Peter Parker was a regular Joe who had problems with money, health, family and dating – as well as the responsibility of being a super hero. Steve Ditko's artwork was like nothing else. As Stan wrote years later: "His layouts and drawings set the

unique illustrative style for the strip, a style that would last for many years to come, a style that made Spidey utterly distinctive among comic strip creations. His sense of pacing, his flair for action scenes, and his ability to make the most outlandish situations look totally believable after he had drawn them gave the early Spider-Man stories an impetus that helped keep them rolling until this very day."[8]

Steve's thin, anxious Spider-Man felt like a real teenager – there were lines of genuine worry on Peter Parker's face. Steve Ditko loved to constantly push the envelope, drawing Peter Parker a supporting cast of realistic but disturbing characters, including the boorish J. Jonah Jameson and the frail Aunt May. Spider-Man was loved by fans because he clearly lived in the real world.

In 1966 Steve Ditko left Marvel, passing the art duties to John Romita Sr., who would draw Spider-Man for the next few years. Steve had already ensured his legacy; his creations would live on for decades, growing and shifting as they found generation after generation of readers.

─────────────────── **KEY TO PLATE** ───────────────────

1: Amazing Fantasy #15
August 1962
Jack Kirby drew the cover for Spider-Man's first appearance, with Steve Ditko providing the interior art.

2: The Amazing Spider-Man #1
March 1963
Steve Ditko's Spider-Man is sharper

and more angular than Jack Kirby's heroes.

3: The Amazing Spider-Man #19
December 1964
Spider-Man was very much part of the Marvel Universe and was friends with the Human Torch.

4: The Amazing Spider-Man #33
February 1966
Coming towards the end of Ditko's run, *The Amazing Spider-Man #33* is seen as one of his most emotionally powerful issues.

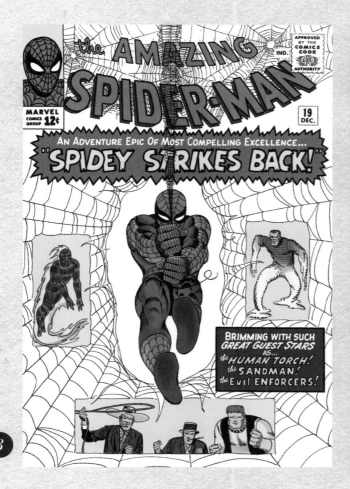

DOCTOR STRANGE

Shortly after Stan Lee and Steve Ditko created Spider-Man they worked together on something very different. In 1963 *Strange Tales* #110 introduced Dr. Stephen Strange, an arrogant surgeon who damaged his hands in a car crash and then studied to become a practitioner of the mystic arts. Doctor Strange lived in the Sanctum Sanctorum, which, like most Marvel locations, was found in New York City.

Doctor Strange never saw the popularity of Spider-Man, and at first was kept to five-page stories at the back of *Strange Tales*, with Doctor Strange's surname coming from the name of the comic. Stan felt that he needed something a little more, later he would write: "I love catchy phrases. It wasn't enough to call him Doctor Strange. I had to add 'Master of the Mystic Arts' to the title."[9] Stan was perhaps not sure about Doctor Strange at first, worrying that he would be too hard to understand. He needn't have worried, as the character would soon find an audience.

The relatively loose working arrangement of Stan's "Marvel Method" of scripting allowed Steve the creative freedom to explore the mind-bending concepts introduced by the character. Doctor Strange traversed impossible psychedelic landscapes filled with precise, rippling details. While the dimensions created by Jack Kirby in *The Fantastic Four* were the huge playgrounds of the gods, Steve Ditko's realms were precise fractals, repeating themselves to infinity. Doctor Strange didn't just fight villains like the dread Dormammu, he fought abstract ideas like Nightmare, the Living Tribunal and Eternity. These mind-blowing stories came from contemporary ideas of psychology and metaphysics, and were unlike anything else at the time.

While Doctor Strange was never the runaway success that Spider-Man was, he found his own audience and grew in popularity over Ditko's run on the title and beyond. The character was especially popular on college campuses and became a sort of counter-culture mascot, even appearing on the cover of Pink Floyd's second album *A Saucerful of Secrets*, released in 1968.

KEY TO PLATE

*1: **Strange Tales #122***
July 1964

While other heroes fought more conventional villains, Doctor Strange battled metaphysical opponents like Nightmare, the Lord of Dreams.

Dr. STRANGE
MASTER OF THE MYSTIC ARTS!
"THE WORLD BEYOND"
featuring: "NIGHTMARE!"
ONCE AGAIN, THE MIGHTY MARVEL GROUP PROUDLY PRESENTS DR. STRANGE, THE WIDELY-ACCLAIMED SMASH SENSATION WHO HAS MADE BLACK MAGIC THE MOST FASCINATING NEW SUBJECT IN COMICDOM!
WRITTEN, WITH A TOUCH OF SORCERY BY....... STAN LEE
DRAWN, WITH A DASH OF NECROMANCY BY....... STEVE DITKO
LETTERED, WITH A NUMBER 6 PEN POINT BY....... ART SIMEK
X-696
1

DAREDEVIL

Spider-Man was an unexpected smash, so Marvel wanted to capitalise on the momentum. *Daredevil* launched in 1964, telling the story of lawyer Matthew Murdock. Matt was blinded in a childhood accident, which gave him other, advanced senses. Matt's father, the boxer Battlin' Jack Murdock, was killed after refusing to throw a boxing match, so Matt assumed the identity of *Daredevil* to track down his killers, sewing together a red-and-yellow outfit and hiding a billy club in his cane.

Daredevil #1 was written by Stan and drawn by veteran comics artist Bill Everett, with Jack Kirby pitching in on character design. Bill Everett had been working for Marvel intermittently since he created the Sub-Mariner in 1939, trying his hand at Captain America and Human Torch comics, as well as various science fiction stories. The first issue of *Daredevil* bursts with action and excitement, with Everett's pencils giving Matt Murdock a lithe, athletic feel. Bill Everett had a full-time job at the time, and the pressure of comics deadlines was too much for him to keep up with, so a new artist was found. *Daredevil #2* was pencilled by Joe Orlando, an artist and editor who has been working on EC's horror comics and *MAD* magazine. Wally Wood (another EC veteran) took over from issue #5 and gave Daredevil his distinctive red costume in issue #7.

Daredevil was very much part of the connected Marvel Universe. He was constantly interacting with other characters – Ben Grimm pops into his office for legal advice in the second issue, and Daredevil battles Spider-Man villain Electro in the same comic. The Marvel Universe felt like a living, breathing thing, with stories branching off in different directions, then meeting up again. The sheer ambition of these interconnected stories would be inconceivable in any other medium, but the sprawling growth of Marvel Comics allowed it to happen.

Stan Lee was surprised to find a new audience for the character, writing years later: "Among my most treasured memories in connection with *Daredevil* are the many letters we've received over the past years, letters from people associated with organisations which aid the handicapped, and particularly the blind. These letters have told of the warm reception given to Daredevil's adventures by handicapped readers, readers who feel they have finally found a hero with whom they can empathise, a hero whose fantastic exploits help to strengthen their own sense of pride and self-esteem."[10]

Daredevil would never achieve the near universal popularity of Spider-Man, but the broader character gave writers and artists a wider canvas to work on. Over the years creators like Frank Miller, Kevin Smith and Brian Michael Bendis have used the character to discuss issues of faith, death, celebrity and forgiveness, perhaps in ways they couldn't with other super heroes.

KEY TO PLATE

*1: **Daredevil #1***
April 1964
The first issue of *Daredevil* promised readers another hero in the style of the hugely popular Spider-Man.

*2: **Daredevil #13***
February 1966

Jack Kirby provided exciting artwork for *Daredevil* covers and interiors once the comic had been launched.

*3: **Daredevil #13***
February 1966
Daredevil has always had some of the most physical fight scenes of

any super hero.

*4: **Daredevil Volume 2 #1***
November 1998
Filmmaker Kevin Smith wrote the groundbreaking "Guardian Devil" storyline.

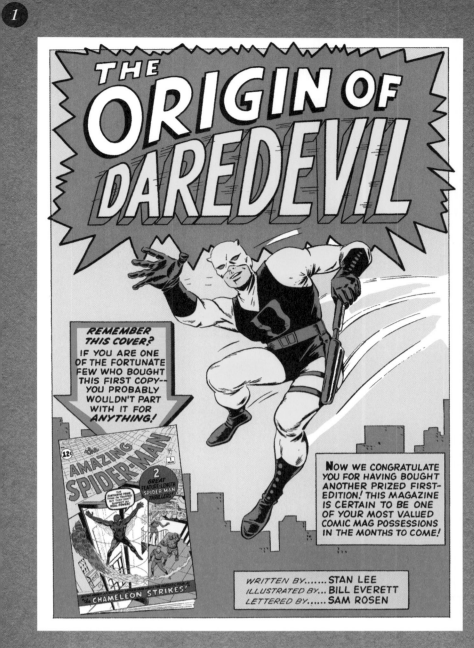

FACE FRONT, TRUE BELIEVERS!

Flo Steinberg
Roy Thomas
The Merry Marvel Marching Society

FLO STEINBERG

Marvel was growing into something bigger than anyone could have hoped. Stan Lee couldn't handle everything on his own, so in 1963 he hired Florence "Flo" Steinberg to be his "gal Friday" – a cross between a PA, a secretary, and a fixer. Flo was a 24-year-old History major who had only recently moved to New York – she didn't know a great deal about comics when she started, but for $65 a week she was willing to learn.

Marvel Comics at the time was essentially Stan Lee. Marvel was published by Martin Goodman's Magazine Management company, and Stan kept a one-man office. Writers like Mario Puzo, Mickey Spillane and Bruce Jay Friedman were all employed as Magazine Management staff writers at one time, all of them wondering about the excitable comics editor who could often be seen jumping on the furniture as he was dictating plots to secretaries. Production manager Sol Brodsky kept the ship running, but Flo was the second full-time Marvel Comics staff member.

Flo soon became indispensable to Marvel. Her wide range of duties included taking notes from Stan, chasing down artwork from artists, replying to every single reader letter, sending artwork to the Comics Code Authority, and also stopping unwanted

1

"AND THIS REALITY'S INVISIBLE GIRL IS ACTUALLY MARVEL COMICS' SECRETARY FLO STEINBERG, BETTER KNOWN UNDER THE SOBRIQUET "FABULOUS FLO.""

2

visitors from entering the Marvel offices. Often she would tell children trying to sneak in that yes, this was where Spider-Man lived, but he was out stopping a robbery at that moment. Marvel received over a hundred letters from fans a day, and Flo made sure that they were all opened and answered.

Flo was such a ubiquitous presence at Marvel that it wasn't long before Stan started referring to her in the letters pages, always as "Fabulous Flo Steinberg". *What If #11* from 1978 even has Flo as a character in the Jack Kirby written story called "What if the Original Marvel Bullpen Had Become the Fantastic Four?", with Flo taking the place of Sue Storm to Stan Lee's Reed Richards.

In 1968 Flo Steinberg left Marvel to work in independent comics, but eventually returned to Marvel in the 1990s as a proofreader, where she worked (at least part time) until her death in 2017.

───────────── **KEY TO PLATE** ─────────────

1: **What If? Vol 1 #11**
October 1978
Everyone in the Marvel Bullpen got their own nickname, and "Fabulous Flo" was no exception.

2: **What If? Vol 1 #11**
October 1978
In an issue of *What If?* comic, Jack Kirby drew the Marvel Bullpen as the Fantastic Four.

3: **What If? Vol 1 #11**
October 1978
Flo and Stan worked closely together for many years.

ROY THOMAS

Roy Thomas was a new breed of Marvel employee — a fan who had been reading Marvel comics for years and now wanted to work in the House of Ideas. "From the day I first laid eyes on (and purchased two copies of) *The Fantastic Four* #1 in 1961, I was a fan of the Lee-Kirby approach to super heroes,"[1] Roy would later write. Roy had written letters regularly to both Marvel and DC Comics, and his letters had been printed in several issues of *The Fantastic Four*. "FF #3 was excellent!" reads his letter in *Fantastic Four* #5. "I've just subscribed to *FF* for two years — I hope it runs much longer than that." An important voice in early Marvel fandom, Roy Thomas was also editor of comics fanzine *Alter Ego*. Roy loved comics.

In 1965, dissatisfied with his job as an English teacher, Roy moved from Jackson, Missouri to New York, looking to break into comics. Roy's test to work at Marvel was simple — write speech balloons over Jack Kirby pages of *The Fantastic Four* comics. Roy passed the test and started almost immediately as Marvel Comics' staff writer and then assistant editor.

As one of Marvel's biggest fans, Roy often knew more about Marvel continuity than anyone else in the building, and Stan would ask Roy questions about the finer details of comics that he had written himself. Roy followed in Stan's footsteps, and Stan began to trust him enough let him loose on the Marvel stable of characters. Roy's first super hero comic was *Iron Man*, and before long he was writing *The Avengers*, *The Fantastic Four*, *Doctor Strange* and *The X-Men*.

In 1972 Stan Lee became publisher of Marvel, so Roy took his place as editor-in-chief, still writing flagship title *The Fantastic Four* as part of his other duties. Roy left Marvel in 1980, but has continued to work for Marvel on various projects ever since.

--- KEY TO PLATE ---

*1: **The Fantastic Four King-Sized Special #5***
November 1967

Jack Kirby wrote and drew this parody of the Marvel Bullpen. Roy Thomas can be seen in the

lower left of the image.

THE MERRY MARVEL MARCHING SOCIETY

Stan knew that the most important thing for Marvel Comics wasn't the super heroes or the large list of titles – it was the fans.

Marvel Comics had a page set aside for a column called "Bullpen Bulletins", where Stan would update the readers about the latest titles and news of the Marvel writers and artists. Even though at first he was the only regular member of staff (joined by Sol Brodsky as a freelance production manager and later by Flo Steinberg), he made the Marvel Bullpen sound like a bustling hive of ideas, where anything was possible. Everyone had nicknames from "Smilin' Stan" (or "Stan the Man") to "Jolly Jack" (or "King Kirby"). Bundles of mail poured in every day, but every letter was answered by "Fabulous Flo Steinberg". Readers felt as if they knew the people who were making their comics.

In 1964 the Merry Marvel Marching Society (also known as the MMMS) was formed, a fan club that would bring readers even closer to the Marvel Bullpen. For $1 members would get a letter, a membership card, a certificate, a badge, a notepad and a record of "The Voices of Marvel". The record featured all the regular Marvel writers, artists and staff (apart from Steve Ditko) telling each other jokes and generally fooling around. The Merry Marvel Marching Society grew to be so popular that it almost became a full-time job just to process all the applications.

As Marvel was growing so quickly, continuity mistakes were bound to slip into the comics, but Stan's genius was making a game of it. Readers who wrote in with errors (and an explanation for why they occurred) would receive a "no-prize". Originally, it was just a mention in the letters pages. Later, Marvel would actually send an envelope with the words "Congratulations! This envelope contains a genuine Marvel Comics NO-PRIZE which you have just won!" which was, of course, empty inside. No-prizes became incredibly popular and were later awarded for charitable works or "meritorious service to the cause of Marveldom".

Marvel fandom spread further than anyone could have hoped to imagine. A 1965 *Esquire* poll ranked Spider-Man and the Hulk equal to Bob Dylan and Che Guevara as favourite revolutionary icons for college students. Stan started to visit college campuses to give talks, which would soon be sold out. Everyone was suddenly talking about Marvel! In 1965 groundbreaking Italian filmmaker Federico Fellini visited the Marvel offices and met Stan, professing to be a huge fan of Marvel Comics. Stan and Fellini stayed in touch, with Stan later visiting Fellini's villa in Rome.

Stan knew that comics wouldn't survive unless fans treated each other well, writing in the letters page of *The Fantastic Four* #24: "It is our intention, here at Marvel, to produce comics which are so well-written and well-drawn that they'll elevate the entire field in the minds of the public! It is up to US, the producers, and YOU, the fans, to make comics something to be proud of."[12]

─────────────── **KEY TO PLATE** ───────────────

1: *Fantastic Four King-Sized Special #5*
November 1967

The Merry Marvel Marching Society members (referred to here as MMMSers) were soon

part of Marvel comics.

SECTION 6

TO ME, MY X-MEN!

The X-Men
The All-New, All-Different X-Men
Dark Phoenix and Beyond
Wolverine

THE X-MEN

The X-Men was initially presented as a standard team super hero book comic, designed to capitalise on the success of *The Fantastic Four*, but it soon became something very different. Introduced in 1963, these were heroes who were hated and scorned just because of the way they were born. Stan's first choice for the title of the comic was *The Mutants*, but the name was changed to *The X-Men* after he was told that no one would understand the word "mutant".

Created by Stan Lee and Jack Kirby, the X-Men were a group of teenagers brought together by Professor Charles Xavier to help control the powers that came from their mutant gene. Rather than go through a whole set of complicated origin stories, Stan opted to make them all mutants for simplicity's sake. Led by the ever-serious Cyclops, the team consisted of the acrobatic Beast, the winged Angel, the frosty Iceman and the telekinetic Marvel Girl.

The X-Men's main nemesis was Magneto, a mutant with the power of magnetism. Magneto believed that mankind and mutants could not coexist, and humans must be wiped off the face of the Earth, while Professor X wanted humans and mutants to live together peacefully.

Soon, these stories about mutants took on a life of their own, and became vehicles for discussing many different societal issues. The battle between the non-violent Professor X and the militant Magneto could be seen in terms of the struggle between Martin Luther King Jr. and Malcolm X. Similarly, the fact that the mutant gene manifested itself at puberty was seen by some as a way to explore LGBT issues. Magneto was revealed to be a survivor of Nazi concentration camps, giving a damaged humanity and a background to his battle against prejudice. "Mutants in the Marvel Universe have always stood as a metaphor for the underclass, the outsiders; they represent the ultimate minority,"[13] explains X-Men writer Chris Claremont.

By the end of the 1960s, however, sales of *The X-Men* were flagging, and while writer Roy Thomas and artist Neal Adams tried to revitalise the comic with new characters like Havok and Polaris, the greatest danger to *The X-Men* was reader apathy. Sales dwindled and from 1970 the X-Men became a reprint title, reusing old issues. But the X-Men were about to mutate.

───────────────────────── **KEY TO PLATE** ─────────────────────────

1: **The Uncanny X-Men #1**
September 1963

The first issue of *The X-Men* pitted a group of superpowered teens

against Magneto, the master of magnestism.

THE ALL-NEW, ALL-DIFFERENT X-MEN

Giant-Size X-Men #1 was a massive mutation for the X-Men. In 1975 writer Len Wein and artist Dave Cockrum started almost completely from the ground up, reimagining the team and the dynamic. When the original team of X-Men are captured by Krakoa the living island, Professor X and Cyclops bring an entirely new team of mutants together to save them.

Everything about the comic felt new, from the oversized page count, to the exciting cover featuring the new and diverse team of heroes ripping their way through a startled image of the original team. The X-Men were no longer white students, they were now a diverse group of adults from all over the world. Some were completely new heroes – like Storm from Africa, Colossus from Russia, Nightcrawler from Germany and the Native-American Thunderbird (who would not survive three issues) – while others like the Sunfire, Banshee and Wolverine (from Japan, Ireland and Canada respectively) had been seen in previous Marvel comics. The diverse team came from an editorial request for a comic that could be sold all over the world, and the inclusive nature of the X-Men is something that has been important to the comic book ever since.

Even the end of the comic was new and different – how would these two teams work together? Who were the X-Men now? Something about this exciting team was incredibly compelling, and over the next few issues readers flocked back to *The X-Men*. Stan Lee later summed it up: "It's almost impossible to read a few issues of *The X-Men* without feeling that each and every one of the mutant heroes has become a close personal friend, because they all have their own distinctive personalities that make you feel you know them, understand them and care about them."[14]

"From the ashes of the past grow the fires of the future," claimed the first page of *Giant-Size X-Men* #1, and writer Len Wein had no idea how right he was. Len Wein plotted the next few issues (*X-Men* #94 and #95) before passing the writing reins to Chris Claremont. One of the most popular runs in the history of Marvel Comics was about to begin.

--- **KEY TO PLATE** ---

*1: **Giant-Size X-Men #1***
May 1975
The new team revealed here would breathe new life into the X-Men.

*2: **Uncanny X-Men #94***
August 1975
The new X-Men soon proved to be just as popular as the previous team.

*3: **Uncanny X-Men #100***
August 1976
Part of the excitement of this era of X-Men was seeing the friction within the team.

DARK PHOENIX AND BEYOND

Within a few years *The X-Men* (now called *The Uncanny X-Men*) went from being a reprint title to one of Marvel's highest-selling comics. Writer Chris Claremont was joined by artist John Byrne, and the spark between the two creators translated directly into sales.

Perhaps the most shocking story of their run was "The Dark Phoenix Saga". In 1980 Jim Shooter was editor-in-chief at Marvel and was keen to keep the popular *The Uncanny X-Men* title as interesting and fresh as possible. Jean Grey had recently been given incredible powers as the Phoenix. "Chris [Claremont] has a story in mind where Phoenix was going to slowly… be corrupted by her power and become a great danger," recalled Shooter in a later interview. "This being Marvel Comics, it wasn't going to be a sham, it was going to be a permanent change in her character – she was going to become evil."[15] Chris Claremont and John Byrne originally worked on a story where the Phoenix murdered a planet of innocent people and was depowered by the Shi'ar. But Jim Shooter read the issue and realised that it didn't feel as if Jean was being sufficiently punished. After a great deal of discussion it was decided: the Phoenix had to die. This was a huge deal – Jean Grey was a Stan Lee creation, and her death made it feel as if anything could happen to the X-Men.

Chris Claremont stayed with *The X-Men* throughout the 1980s, working with the creative team to build *The Uncanny X-Men* to be one of Marvel's most popular and exciting titles. The X-Men were joined by X-Factor (initially formed from the original X-Men team), the European team Excalibur and the younger New Mutants (who became X-Force). In 1991 a companion title was launched, titled simply *X-Men*, which was written by Chris Claremont and drawn and co-plotted by hotshot artist Jim Lee. The new *X-Men* #1 was a legitimate phenomenon and still holds the Guinness World Record for the best-selling comic book of all time.

Former *X-Men* editor Louise Simonson knew what made the comic work, saying: "If there is a theme to these *Uncanny X-Men* issues, it is transformation. This idea… like a repeated melody, is one of the things that has made X-Men stories so effective, affecting, and impossible to ignore."[16] However, the key messages of the X-Men, of diversity, acceptance and bravery, are ones that never change.

KEY TO PLATE

*1: **The Uncanny X-Men #135***
July 1980
Phoenix versus the X-Men.

*2: **The Uncanny X-Men #136***
August 1980

*3: **The Uncanny X-Men #137***
September 1980
Phoenix must die!

*4: **The Uncanny X-Men #137***
September 1980
Jean Grey's final moments.

*5: **X-Men #1***
September 1991
A new era of X-Men!

*6: **X-Men #1***
September 1991
The best-selling comic book of all time.

WOLVERINE

Wolverine's first appearance in *The Incredible Hulk* #181 (technically, he appears in the final panel of issue #180) in 1974 did not provide many clues for how incredibly popular the character would become. Veteran Marvel artist John Romita Sr. designed the character, while penciller Herb Trimpe and writer Len Wein created the first issue. "If you really want to tangle with someone," growls Logan, "why not try your luck against – the Wolverine?" In the issue, Wolverine is an agent of the Canadian government, a scrappy mutant with unbreakable, Adamantium-laced claws. Readers would learn in later comics that he had heightened senses, Adamantium bones and a mutant healing factor. At first he seemed like a fine sparring partner for the Hulk, but there was not a lot to differentiate him from other single-issue antagonists.

Logan returned in *Giant-Size X-Men* #1 in 1975 and was part of the new ongoing X-Men team. Again, Wolverine's full potential wasn't immediately obvious and it wasn't until Canadian artist and co-plotter John Byrne joined the team that Wolverine was given more of a backstory. Something in Wolverine's dark and brooding nature connected with fans, and soon he was popular enough for his own comic, which often featured other X-Men including Kitty Pryde.

Logan's origins were initially vague and mysterious – a Canadian government agent known as Weapon X, he was unable to remember much of his past. In 1991 the "Weapon X" story in *Marvel Comics Presents* by Barry Windsor-Smith filled in the details about the shadowy government programme that added Adamantium to Logan's bones and turned him into a brain-washed killer. In 2001 "Origin" told even more of his story – Wolverine was actually born James Howlett, the sickly son of rich Canadian farm owners (though possibly the illegitimate son of the groundskeeper, Thomas Logan), who fled his home after his mutant powers manifested themselves.

The breakout star of the X-Men, Wolverine was soon appearing in other super hero teams and did stints in Alpha Flight, the Avengers and X-Force. He has had the Adamantium stripped from his bones, was reunited with his estranged son, adopted a young female clone of himself and died more than once. Wolverine's complex and tortured nature has evolved to make him one of Marvel's most interesting tough guys, and has made him one of the most popular super heroes in the world.

———————————— KEY TO PLATE ————————————

1: The Incredible Hulk #181
November 1974
In his first appearance Wolverine fought the Hulk and battled Wendigo.

2: Wolverine #2
October 1982
In this story Wolverine's journey to Japan revealed secrets from his past.

4: X-Men #11
August 1992
Wolverine became one of the most popular members of the X-Men.

3: Marvel Comics Presents #83
August 1991
"Weapon X" revealed the horrors that Logan had been subjected to.

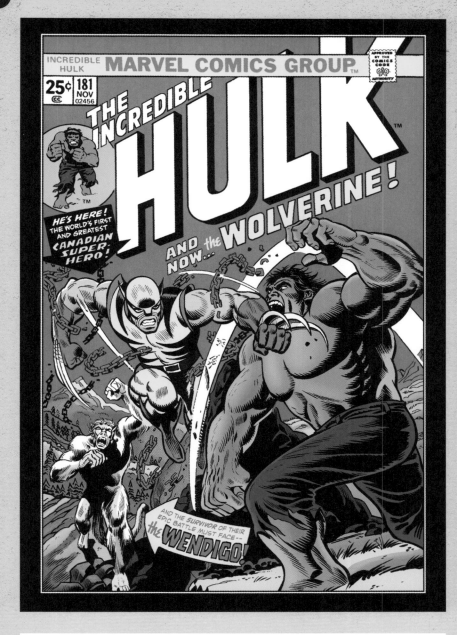

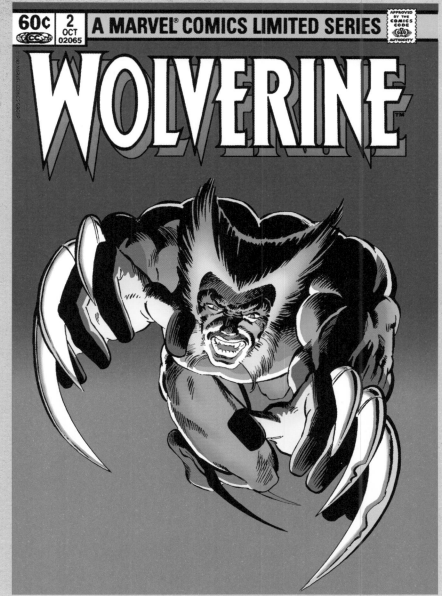

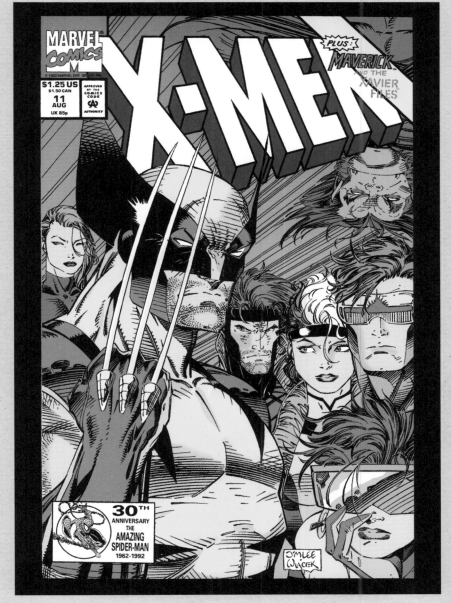

SECTION 7

A NEW KIND OF HERO

The Punisher
Captain Marvel
Ghost Rider
Blade

THE PUNISHER

"The most lethal hired assassin ever! His assignment: KILL SPIDER-MAN!" screamed *The Amazing Spider-Man* #129, announcing the first appearance of the Punisher. A former marine, Frank Castle waged a one-man war on crime after his family was killed by underworld hitmen. "I needed a disposable character to be front-and-center for a one-issue confrontation with Spider-Man," explained writer Gerry Conway. "The early 1970s were a dark time, with vigilantes on the street, and corruption in high places. I thought it might be fun for Spider-Man to face a modern vigilante who'd been manipulated by [bad guy] the Jackal into believing Spidey's negative press."[17]

Frank Castle's distinctive death's head skull emblem was initially much smaller in Gerry Conway's concept drawing, but art director John Romita Sr. asked for it to be made much larger, and in artist Ross Andru's finished pages it covers the Punisher's entire chest. "The Punisher" was already a name taken for one of Galactus' minions, but Stan Lee thought it fitted this new vigilante much better. The Comics Code Authority at the time had very strict guidelines about heroes killing people, so the Punisher initially used a non-lethal "concussion rifle", and later carried guns that fired special "mercy bullets", which knocked out his opponents without killing them. His non-lethal ways didn't last long, and these days he guns down bad guys without a second thought.

The Punisher's popularity took his creators by surprise, and soon he was appearing with bigger characters such as Captain America and Daredevil. Frank Castle was a new and different type of comic character, a tortured anti-hero who was on a much darker and more personal mission than many of the heroes at the time.

Frank has had several comics of his own, including *The Punisher*, *The Punisher: War Zone* and *The Punisher: War Journal*. In 2003 the series *Born* by Garth Ennis and Darick Robertson told the story of Frank's time during the Vietnam War, and how the seething violence of the Punisher was always just below the surface of Frank Castle.

The Punisher has had many allies in his campaign, including members of the police, FBI, CIA and S.H.I.E.L.D., but his most consistent associate has been Microchip. Dave Lieberman was a computer hacker whose nephew was killed by the Kingpin, so David started helping the Punisher. Microchip kept Frank supplied with guns, money and plans for years, but the two eventually ended up falling out over the Punisher's extreme methods.

With his distinctive skull emblem, no-nonsense approach to crime and unflinching moral certainty, the Punisher is part of the darker side of Marvel. The Punisher is popular in a troubled and morally-conflicted society because he is always completely sure about what he is doing — his only powers are his military training, his determination and his utter unwillingness to compromise.

─────────────── KEY TO PLATE ───────────────

*1: **The Punisher #1***
July 1987

The Punisher has always been one of Marvel's most extreme characters,

an unstoppable force in his war against crime.

MARVEL
#1 FIRST ISSUE OF AN UNLIMITED SERIES!
THE PUNISHER
75¢ US
95¢ CAN
1
JULY
02860
APPROVED BY THE COMICS CODE AUTHORITY
JANSON '86

1

CAPTAIN MARVEL

The Captain Marvel name is a torch that has been passed to several characters in the Marvel Universe, each with widely different backgrounds. The first Marvel hero to carry the name was an alien called Mar-Vell, who came from a race known as the Kree. Created by Stan Lee and Gene Colan in 1967, Captain Mar-Vell soon rebelled against his Kree superiors and became Earth's protector. The character was revamped several times over the next decade, before dying in Marvel's first original graphic novel: 1982's *The Death of Captain Marvel*. Written and painted by Jim Starlin, whose father had recently died of cancer, the graphic novel is a powerful exploration of death, loss and acceptance.

Monica Rambeau was the second character to take the name Captain Marvel, and was a complete sea-change from her Kree predecessor. A strong, confident black woman, in her first panel we see Monica setting off Peter Parker's spider-sense because of her extraordinary powers. A former New Orleans harbour patrol lieutenant, this Captain Marvel was transformed into a being of energy when she smashed a villain's energy disruptor. Monica joined the Avengers and eventually became team leader. After problems with her powers, Monica gave up the Captain Marvel name, becoming Photon then Pulsar and later Spectrum.

Carol Danvers had been part of the Marvel Universe for nearly as long as Mar-Vell himself. In Mar-Vell's second appearance he met Ms. Danvers, who was head of security on the Cape Kennedy missile base that happened to be holding a giant alien robot. Carol disappeared from comics for a while after being caught in a Kree device called a Pysche-Magnetron, but returned in 1977 in her own title and with new Kree-based powers. *Ms. Marvel*, written by Gerry Conway with art from John Romita Sr., was designed to be at the forefront of the feminist movement; Carol Danvers is now a magazine editor working for J. Jonah Jameson, splitting her time between battling bad guys and fighting for equal pay. *Ms. Marvel* was intended in some way to open up the male-dominated comics industry to women. "Almost without our intending it," explained Gerry Conway, "this book was a sign at the bottom of the treehouse that said, in the mildest possible way, 'Girls Allowed'." [18]

Ms. Marvel joined the Avengers, and became a semi-regular guest star in *The Uncanny X-Men* during Chris Claremont's run. Carol gained new powers, a new look and a new super hero name: Binary. After she lost these powers she took on the name Warbird, before reverting to Ms. Marvel.

In 2012 Marvel launched a new *Captain Marvel* comic written by Kelly Sue DeConnick with art from Dexter Soy. Carol took on the Captain Marvel name after being encouraged to honour her mentor Mar-Vell by Captain America. This new Captain Marvel had a bold new look and a human heart — a powerhouse with a longing to explore the stars..

KEY TO PLATE

1: Captain Marvel #1
May 1968
The first Captain Marvel (real name Mar-Vell) was friends with Carol Danvers.

2: The Amazing Spider-Man Annual #16
January 1982
Monica Rambeau was the second Captain Marvel, and later became The Avengers' leader.

3: Ms. Marvel #1
January 1977
Carol Danver's first super hero identity was Ms. Marvel.

4: Captain Marvel (2012) #1
July 2012
Carol Danver's Captain Marvel costume was designed by artist Jamie McKelvie, drawn here by Ed McGuinness.

GHOST RIDER

The concept for Ghost Rider was initially pitched by writer Gary Friedrich as a revamp for the Evel Knievel-themed *Daredevil* villain The Stuntmaster. The idea of a demonic motorbike rider was decided by editor-in-chief Roy Thomas to be too cool to be a bit-part villain, so artist Mike Ploog was put to work to draw a new hero called Ghost Rider in 1972's *Marvel Spotlight #5*.

Marvel had already published a Western comic named *Ghost Rider* about a masked cowboy dressed in white, but this new character was very different. Johnny Blaze was a daredevil motorcycle stuntman who had made a pact with the devil! "You will walk the Earth as my emissary in the dark hours," the devil taunted, while giving Johnny Blaze his trademark flaming skull and motorbike. The Ghost Rider has one of Marvel's most brilliant and distinctive looks, combining demonic hellfire with circus spectacle. Over the years he has gained powers beyond his burning head and vehicle – perhaps his most striking is the Penance Stare, which forces the victim to endure all the pain that they have caused other people.

Johnny Blaze fought supernatural evil in his own comic for several years, using his supernatural abilities to punish the wicked. Johnny Blaze's soul had been bonded with the demon Spirit of Vengeance called Zarathos, and after a long battle Johnny was finally able to rid himself of the curse of being Ghost Rider. Johnny later returned as a shotgun-wielding demon hunter and later took on the mantle of the Ghost Rider once again.

Various other characters have been Ghost Rider. Danny Ketch was the Ghost Rider for most of the 1990s, a young man who gained his powers when he touched the glowing gas cap of a mysterious motorcycle. Danny's powers were much the same as Johnny's and it was later revealed that the two were long-lost brothers. More recently Robbie Reyes, a Mexican-American high-school student, has taken on the role. Reyes' Ghost Rider drives a car instead of a motorcycle and has a polished metal flaming head instead of a floating skull.

Ghost Rider is a dark and powerful hero. Like the Punisher he refuses to hurt anyone he deems innocent, but uses the full force of his powers to punish guilty souls. He always manages to maintain an air of supernatural mystery, his demonic face hiding all human emotions.

KEY TO PLATE

*1: **Marvel Spotlight #5***
August 1972

Ghost Rider allowed Marvel to tell darker, supernatural stories.

BLADE

Due to changes in the Comics Code Authority, horror comics started to come back into fashion in the 1970s, bringing hordes of werewolves, vampires and monsters back to the newsstand. Marvel was never a company to miss out on a trend, and launched *The Tomb of Dracula* in 1972. A vampire comic is nothing without a vampire hunter, and Blade was introduced in *The Tomb of Dracula #10*, written by Marv Wolfman and pencilled by Gene Colan. Blade is initially presented as a street-talking warrior – his bandolier of stakes is held over a green leather jacket and he sports an afro and yellow wraparound sunglasses. Gene Colan's pencils give Blade a tough, physical look. "Maybe you're hot-stuff back in Transylvania, but nobody messes around with Blade – the Vampire-Slayer!" he taunts Dracula in his first appearance.

His character was fleshed out more in the black-and-white anthology title *Vampire Tales #8*, which told of how Blade's mother was killed while delivering him by a vampire who would later be revealed to be Deacon Frost. Blade, real name Eric Brooks, was born in 1929 in London and had dedicated his life to finding the vampire that had killed his mother. Due to the unnatural circumstances surrounding his birth, Blade was born with an enzyme in his blood that made him immune to vampire bites and mind control.

Blade reappeared in the 1990s as part of Marvel's *Rise of the Midnight Sons* crossover, sporting a new look but with the same determination for killing vampires. The afro and wraparound shades were gone, but the leather jacket and fearless sneer were still very much present. Now a member of the supernatural Nightstalkers team, Blade's weapon of choice was a specially treated samurai sword.

A 1998 blockbuster movie starring Wesley Snipes reinvigorated interest in the character, and Blade fought vampires in his own comic. Blade's abilities were changed in *Peter Parker: Spider-Man #9* in 1999 when he was bitten by Moribus, the living vampire. Normal vampire bites have no effect on Blade, but Moribus got his vampirism from a failed biochemical experiment, so his bite gave Blade various vampire strengths without making him susceptible to sunlight. This turned Blade into "the Daywalker", a vampire who can come out during the day.

Despite claiming to prefer to work alone, Blade has been a member of several super hero teams, even joining the Avengers when they were up against an army of vampires. The fact that he was born in the UK gave him membership to the Captain Britain's MI-13 team.

KEY TO PLATE

1: *The Tomb of Dracula #10*
July 1973
Blade's look has changed over the years, but his no-nonsense attitude to vampires has not.

2: *The Tomb of Dracula #10*
July 1973
From his first appearance Blade was afraid of no one, not even Dracula.

3: *Blade: Sins of the Father #1*
October 1998
Blade's look has changed to keep up with the times.

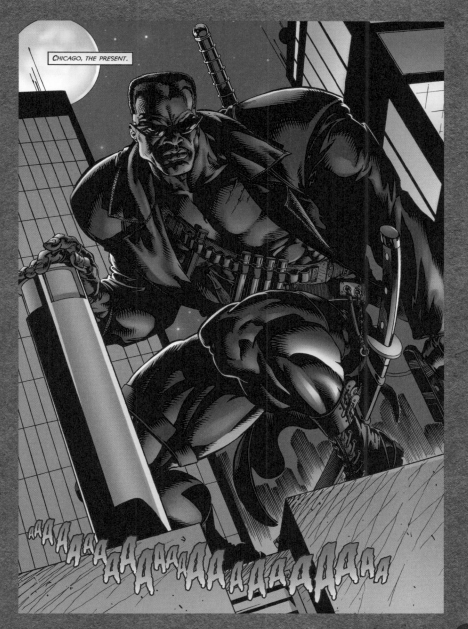

SECTION 8

PROTECTING THE GALAXY

The Guardians of the Galaxy
Thanos
The Infinity Stones

THE GUARDIANS OF THE GALAXY

The Guardians of the Galaxy is a name that has been taken by different teams in the Marvel Universe, often separated by galaxies, dimensions and millennia. The first team was introduced by writer Arnold Drake and artist Gene Colan in *Marvel Super-Heroes* #18 in 1969, and were a time-travelling group of warriors from the 30th century. Charlie-27 from the planet Jupiter, Martinex from Pluto and Yondu from Centauri-IV joined Earth astronaut Vance Astro to fight evil aliens called the Badoon. After various adventures with the Avengers, the Guardians of the Galaxy finally got their own comic in 1990, which lasted for 69 issues.

Meanwhile, Groot first appeared in *Tales to Astonish* #13 in 1960, a Lee-Kirby monster-of-the-week, who had a considerably larger vocabulary and worse temper than he would have in later appearances. Peter Quill, Star-Lord, was a cocky astronaut first seen in *Marvel Preview* #4 driven to avenge the death of his mother by Badoon soldiers. Rocket was originally conceived by Bill Mantlo and Keith Giffen in *Marvel Preview* #7 in 1976. Rocket made a few guest appearances in *Hulk* and *She-Hulk*, but apart from his own limited series in 1985 he kept a fairly low profile for the next few years. Drax and Gamora were both members of the Infinity Watch, a team formed to keep the Infinity Stones in check. Drax the Destroyer was once a human named Arthur Douglas, transformed after his family was killed by Thanos. Gamora was the adopted daughter of Thanos, but Drax and Gamora learned to work together as teammates.

These five disparate characters were not brought together until 2008 as part of the universe-spanning "Annihilation" saga. Writers Dan Abnett and Andy Lanning created a team of misfits drawn from Marvel's extensive history – Star-Lord, Groot, Rocket, Gamora and Drax share a love of adventure, the need for justice and an inability to fit in anywhere else. They are destined to save the universe, but not to listen to each other very often while they do it.

Various other heroes have joined the Guardians, with Marvel stalwarts like Iron Man, Ant-Man and the Thing all being brief members. The Guardians of the Galaxy may seem loose and wild, but they are a strong, superpowered team dedicated to stopping any threat to the galaxy. As Dan Abnett and Andy Lanning put it, they are "a hard-hitting, proactive team prepared to jump headlong into the flames and make sure that future cataclysms… get headed off at the pass. It's a dirty job, but somebody's got to do it. Those bodies are the Guardians of the Galaxy."[19]

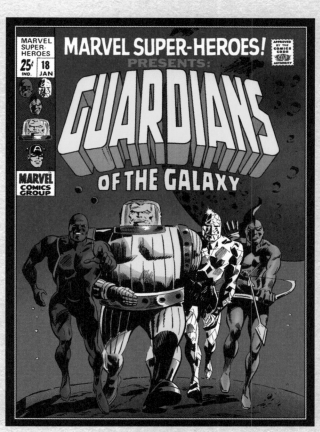

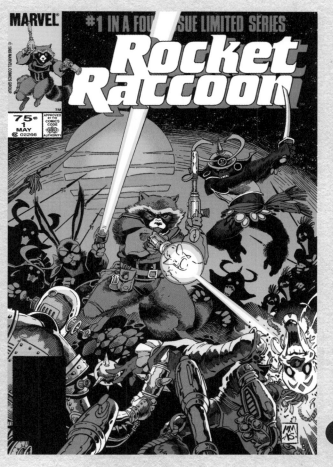

KEY TO PLATE

1: *Tales to Astonish #13*
November 1960
In his first appearance Groot is much more eloquent and much angrier than in later stories.

2: *Marvel Preview #11*
July 1977
One man against a galactic empire!

3: *Marvel Super-Heroes #18*
January 1969
The first Guardians team included Charlie-27, Yondu, Martinex and Major Vance Astro.

4: *Rocket Raccoon #1*
May 1985
Rocket's early adventures were subtitled "Animal Crackers".

THANOS

One of the most dramatic villains in comics, Thanos has long cast a shadow over the Marvel Universe. Created by Jim Stalin, Thanos was first conceived as a galactic tyrant bent on domination, but was later revealed to be in love with the personification of Death itself. Pleasing Mistress Death is Thanos' ultimate goal.

In *The Invincible Iron Man* #55, Thanos is a member of an alien race known as the Titans. The son of the leader known as Mentor, Thanos was banished for his cruelty and is now the leader of a brutish interstellar army. He describes himself as "Thanos the First", and only wants revenge and power. It isn't until later that Thanos' infatuation with Death is revealed, making him a much darker and more complex character. For many of his early appearances he was locked in battle with either Captain Mar-Vell or Adam Warlock, a synthetic humanoid who was created to be the perfect man.

For someone who worships Death, Thanos values his time with the living and has had a lot of different allies over the years. He adopted Gamora, the last of a species called the Zen-Whoberi, and trained her to be an almost unstoppable assassin. Though Thanos was not particularly paternal to Gamora, his methods were undeniably effective. Thanos later brought together a superpowered cosmic team called the Black Order. The team consisted of Proxima Midnight (the mistress of hand-to-hand combat), Corvus Glaive (her husband and Thanos' second-in-command), Black Dwarf (a giant with impenetrable skin), and Ebony Maw (powerful in mind-control). The Black Order were one of the most powerful forces in the galaxy, nearly impossible to defeat.

As a character Thanos has moved from being a simple intergalactic tyrant to something more sinister and disturbing. The reason that Thanos scares so many heroes is that they know he will not be happy until every last being in the universe is dead.

KEY TO PLATE

1: Iron Man #55
February 1973
Drax and Thanos both appear for the first time in this Iron Man issue.

2: Captain Marvel #28
September 1973
Thanos is one of the most powerful and ruthless beings in Marvel comics.

3: The Infinity Gauntlet #4
October 1991
The Infinity Saga saw Thanos finally get control of the Infinity Stones.

4: The Infinity Gauntlet #6
December 1991
The paradox of Thanos is that there is a part of him that yearns for a

peaceful, simple life.

5: Marvel Two-In-One Annual #2
December 1977
Thanos is powerful enough to take on anyone in the Marvel Universe.

1

2

3

4

THE INFINITY STONES

The Infinity Gems (later known as the Infinity Stones) were slowly introduced to the Marvel Universe, starting with the Soul Gem. At first the full power of the Stones was not explained. Later in *The Thanos Quest*, Thanos discovered that the six Infinity Stones are hugely powerful artefacts older than time itself. Separately they give their owners powers over the soul, the mind, time, space, power and reality, but when collected together they create a feedback loop, giving whoever holds them unlimited power.

Thanos first tried to bring the Infinity Stones together in *The Avengers Annual #7* with the express intention of destroying every single star in the galaxy, but was stopped by the Avengers, Spider-Man and the Thing. The Stones were collected and hidden by galactic beings known as the Elders of the Universe, but Thanos tracked them down once again. Thanos' biggest achievement was to collect all the Infinity Gems and wield them in a specially constructed Infinity Gauntlet. With this incredible power he was able to remove half the life from the universe in the blink of an eye during *The Infinity Gauntlet* saga — despite every single Marvel hero (and every cosmic being) coming together to try to stop him. *The Infinity Gauntlet* comics are remarkable because of the sheer desperation of the heroes. Everyone has come together, and nothing — *nothing* — can be done in the face of The Infinity Stones. Eventually Thanos was undone because of his cruelty. He had kept the space pirate Nebula as a disfigured, zombie-like pet, and while Thanos was distracted Nebula was able to take the gauntlet from him and restore the balance of the universe.

For a while the Stones were held by the Illuminati, a collection of heroes including Reed Richards, Tony Stark and Professor Xavier, who met behind the scenes to ensure the smooth running of the Marvel Universe. More recently they have gained sentience, roaming the galaxy and choosing their owners. The Infinity Stones have had many owners, but for Thanos they represent something greater than even the ultimate power in the universe — they give him a chance to impress his greatest love, Death herself.

The reason that the Infinity Stones work so well as a concept is that they are a reflection of the best things about Marvel stories. Marvel comics have great power, they are grounded in reality, they jump between lots of different times and spaces, they feature some of the greatest minds around, and most importantly — they have soul.

———————————————— **KEY TO PLATE** ————————————————

1: **The Thanos Quest #2**
January 1990

Very few people are strong enough to
be able to control the Infinity Stones.

LIBRARY

Index
References

INDEX

REFERENCES

1   Lee, S. and Everett, B. 1991. *Marvel Masterworks 17, Daredevil, Volume 1.* New York: Marvel, pp. 28.

2   Lee, S., Kirby, J. and Ditko, S. 1989. *Marvel Masterworks 8, The Incredible Hulk Volume 1.* New York: Marvel, pp. 7.

3   Lee, S. and Kirby, J. 1993. *Marvel Masterworks 18, The Mighty Thor, Volume 1.* New York: Marvel, pp. 6.

4   Lee, S. and Colan, G. 2008. *Marvel Masterworks 93: Captain America, Volume 4.* New York: Marvel, pp. 8.

5   Lee, S. and Kirby, J. 2000. *Marvel Masterworks 28: The Fantastic Four, Volume 6.* New York: Marvel, pp. 8.

6   Lee, S. and Heck, D. 2005. *Marvel Masterworks 45, Invincible Iron Man, Volume 2.* New York: Marvel, pp. 7.

7   Lee, S., Kirby, J. and Heck, D. 1990. *Marvel Masterworks 4, The Avengers, Volume 1.* New York: Marvel, pp. 6.

8   Lee, S. and Ditko, S. 1987. *Marvel Masterworks 1, The Amazing Spider-Man, Volume 1.* New York: Marvel, pp. 8.

9   Lee, S. and Ditko, S. 1992. *Marvel Masterworks 23, Doctor Strange, Volume 2.* New York: Marvel, pp. 8.

10   Lee, S. and Everett, B. 1991. *Marvel Masterworks 17, Daredevil, Volume 1.* New York: Marvel, pp. 6.

11   Lee, S., Thomas, R. and Kirby, J. 2004. *Marvel Masterworks 38, Avengers, Volume 4.* New York: Marvel, pp. 6.

12   Lee, S. 1964. *Fantastic Four #24.* New York: Marvel, pp. 23.

13   Claremont, C and Anderson, B. 1982. *X-Men: God Loves, Man Kills.* New York: Marvel, pp. 4.

14   Lee, S. and Kirby, J. 1989. *Marvel Masterworks 11, Uncanny X-Men Omnibus, Volume 1.* New York: Marvel, pp. 6.

15   Claremont, C. and Byrne, J. 1984. *Phoenix: The Untold Story #1.* New York: Marvel, pp. 43.

16   Claremont, C. and Byrne, J. 2015. *Marvel Masterworks 214, The Uncanny X-Men Omnibus, Volume 9.* New York: Marvel, pp.8.

17   Conway, G., and Kane, G. 2011. *Marvel Masterworks 155, The Amazing Spider-Man, Volume 13.* New York: Marvel, pp. 8.

18   Conway, G. and Buscema, J. 2014. *Marvel Masterworks 211, Ms. Marvel Volume 1.* New York: Marvel, pp. 8.

19   Abnett, D., Lanning, A., Raney, T. and Wellinton, A. 2008. *Annihilation: Conquest #6.* New York: Marvel, pp. 38.